W9-BAM-022

OPENNESS
IN
ADOPTION

OPENNESS
IN
ADOPTION
New Practices, New Issues

Ruth G. McRoy
Harold D. Grotevant
Kerry L. White

PRAEGER

New York
Westport, Connecticut
London

Library of Congress Cataloging-in-Publication Data

McRoy, Ruth G.
    Openness in adoption : new practices, new issues / Ruth G. McRoy,
Harold D. Grotevant, Kerry L.White.
        p.   cm.
    Bibliography: p.
    Includes index.
    ISBN 0-275-92933-7 (alk. paper)
    1. Adoption—United States—Case studies.   I. Grotevant, Harold
D.   II. White, Kerry L.   III. Title.
HV875.55.M39 1988
362.7'34'0973—dc19   88-2471

Library of Congress Catalog Card Number: 88-2471
ISBN: 0-275-92933-7

First published in 1988

Praeger Publishers, One Madison Avenue, New York, NY 10010
A division of Greenwood Press, Inc.

Printed in the United States of America

∞™

The paper used in this book complies with the
Permanent Paper Standard issued by the National
Information Standards Organization (Z39.48-1984).

10 9 8 7 6 5 4 3 2 1

Contents

Preface

This book serves two functions. It presents the most comprehensive discussion of the issues involved in open adoptions yet available. In addition, it presents the findings of a pilot project designed to assess the consequences of openness in adoption for birthparents and adoptive parents. The study originated in the fall of 1984, when Lutheran Social Service of Texas requested an evaluation of the consequences of openness in adoption, as practiced by three regional offices of the agency.

Seventeen adoptive families and their corresponding birthparents were interviewed between May and September of 1985. In addition, the research team visited and interviewed staff from three regional offices of Lutheran Social Service of Texas and The Edna Gladney Maternity Home. Data were also collected from Catholic Social Services of Green Bay, Wisconsin; the Child Saving Institute of Omaha, Nebraska; and Catholic Social Services for Montana.

This book includes a literature review on confidentiality and openness in adoption, a review of relevant theoretical perspectives, discussion of agency practices, description of research methods utilized, and results and conclusions of the study.

Funding for this study was provided by Lutheran Social Service of Texas. However, the conclusions expressed in this book are solely those of the authors and do not necessarily reflect the official position of the agency.

We wish to express our appreciation to the Reverend Calvin O. Goerdel, Vice President for Social Services; Jean Blankenship, Associate Vice President for Social Services; and the staff of the Austin, Corpus Christi, and San Antonio regional offices of Lutheran Social Service for their cooperation, enthusiasm, and support. We also thank our staff members, Susan Ayers-Lopez, Deborah Fisher, Ann Furuta, Vivian Jenkins, Mary Moran, Katy Mueller, and Steve Satterwhite for assisting with the preparation of this book. We especially thank the adoptive families and birthparents who shared their experiences and perspectives with us.

1
Adoption Issues: Confidentiality in Adoption

Adoption is a sensitive and complex process whereby a child, most often an infant, is permanently incorporated into a family into which he or she is not born. This lifelong process serves a dual purpose. First, it satisfies both legally and socially a married couple's desire to raise a child; second, it provides a home for a child whose birthparents are unable or unwilling to rear it.

It is difficult to quote accurate annual statistics on adoption in the United States because there has been no standard mandatory reporting by states since 1971 (Brieland, Costin, & Atherton, 1980; Kadushin, 1974). In addition, the adoption process itself is both highly structured and secretive. Yet, the number of adoptions in the United States is greater than the total for the rest of the world (Sorosky, Baran, & Pannor, 1978). In 1974, Kadushin estimated that there were 1.5 million adopted children in the United States, or about 2 percent of the total child population. In 1982, 36 percent, or over 91,000, of the 141,861 U.S. adoptions were nonrelative (independent, public, and private agencies) adoptions (National Committee for Adoption [NCFA], 1985).

There has been much speculation on the subject of adoption, including parental motives for adopting (Andrews, 1979; Humphrey, 1969; Krugman, 1967) and the psychodynamics involved in the parent-child adjustment to the special adoptive situation (Andrews, 1978; Brinich, 1980; Brinich & Brinich, 1982; Easson, 1973; Schwartz, 1970; Toussing, 1971). For example, Andrews (1978, 1979) states that adoption has never been an entirely rational process, but "a highly subjective, emotional experience" owing to prevailing societal attitudes about it. She notes that, although adoption as a social institution has won community acceptance, it is still considered second best to build a family through adoption, and that adoptive parents really do not have children of their *own*. Brinich (1980) and Brinich and Brinich (1982) suggest that in human terms, adoption is "always painful and potentially traumatic" because it implies two important social failures: first, that a child is unwanted; and second, that a couple has been unable to conceive. Thus, "the psychopathological potential" of these failures is great.

Beyond the speculations, however, there has been very little examination of longer-term adjustment issues (McRoy & Zurcher, 1983) and of adoptive-family relationships. H. D. Kirk (1959, 1964, 1981) is one of a few researchers who has explored both the meaning and consequences of being an adoptive parent or child. He proposes that adoptive parenting should be recognized as different in some respects and that adoptive parents suffer from a role handicap.

There has also been much written in the literature about numerous issues in adoption practice, including confidentiality versus adoptees' rights to know about their birthparents (Campbell, 1979; Cliff, 1983; Harrington, 1979; Foster, 1979; Lifton, 1975, 1979; Sanders & Sitterly, 1981; Zeilinger, 1979). However, there is almost a total lack of research on the impact of opening the sealed birth records of adoptive triad members (Geissinger, 1984) and on the impact of more openness in adoption agency practice (Kraft, Palombo, Mitchell, Woods, Schmidt, & Tucker, 1985; Belbas, 1987).

Given this lack of knowledge, it is the purpose of this book to examine the issues involved in openness in adoption and the impact of open-adoption practices on the parties concerned. In the first two chapters, the literature on open adoption will be reviewed, and the controversies surrounding this new practice will be explored. Chapter 3 will review the issues involved in openness from six theoretical perspectives. Chapter 4 will present profiles of seven adoption agencies across the United States and their experiences with varying degrees of openness. Chapters 5–9 present the results and implications of a small, pilot study of openness, conducted by the authors, and the book concludes with a commentary by the Reverend Calvin O. Goerdel, Vice President for Social Services, Lutheran Social Service of Texas.

Currently, there is growing debate among adoptees, adoptive parents, birthparents, social workers, and family attorneys over opening sealed adoption records, and on the growing trend toward more openness in adoption practice. There is much public interest in maintaining and strengthening the institution of adoption and in safeguarding the basic rights of individuals. However, research has failed thus far to provide much-needed answers to the following questions: Is it a basic human right to know one's identity? Do birthparents have the right to privacy? How much confidentiality and/or openness is necessary to the well-being of the adoptive families and to the adoption process?

Confidentiality, a characteristic of adoption in western societies, is not present in other societies (Geissinger, 1984; Sachdev, 1984). For example, the Hawaiian and Eskimoan cultures have practiced openness in adoption for centuries (Baran, Pannor, & Sorosky, 1976). Children adopted in these cultures are told who their biological parents are and, in most cases, have met and know all about them.

However, social workers and adoptive parents in the United States traditionally have insisted upon a policy promoting confidentiality in adoption practice. As early as 1917, Minnesota passed the first state law barring public inspection of adoption records (Watson, 1979). By 1950, most states had passed adoption legislation sealing adoption records. The main reasons for this legislation stemmed from such issues as the stigma of illegitimacy, the need for anonymity of parties in-

volved in adoption, and the need for completely severing adoptees' ties to birthparents.

At the time records were sealed, and until very recently, the
prevailing viewpoint has been that normal, well adjusted individuals would not—and should not—need to know any parents other than those who raised them. This attitude is deeply
embedded in U.S. culture where greater emphasis is placed on
immediate blood kin (such as parents and children) than on
more distant relations (Kraft et al., 1985b; Sachdev, 1984). In
1975, Great Britain passed a law that allowed adoptees to have
free access to their original birth records. However, no similar
legislation has been passed in the United States. Kirk and
McDaniel (1984) attribute this major difference in policy to
the way adoption is viewed in both countries. Great Britain
views the adoptive family as uniquely different from the birth
family, with special strengths and weaknesses. In the United
States, there is a perception that adopted children must become integrated into the family to such an extent that no difference exists between them and the family's birthchildren.
The adoptee's original birth records are sealed and made vir-
tually inaccessible without a court order.

Nevertheless, most researchers agree that adopted children
may have problems in their search for identity because they
do not receive adequate information about their biological
parents (Brinich, 1980; Colon, 1978; Seglow, Pringle, & Wedge,
1972; Sorosky, Baran, & Pannor, 1974, 1975, 1978; Triseliotis, 1973). These researchers hold that their developing sense
of identity is incomplete until information about their biological origins is integrated. In 1975, Sorosky, Baran, and Pannor reviewed the literature on genealogical concerns and iden-
tity-crisis development in adopted individuals. They found a
consensus in these studies that adoptees are more vulnerable
than nonadoptees to identity problems developing in adolescence and young adulthood. After interviewing 50 adult adoptees who had recently been reunited with their birthparents,
Sorosky et al. (1975) reported that many of these adoptees
had experienced uncomfortable or delayed revelations about
their backgrounds. They concluded that adoptees may feel a
greater lack of biological connection and continuity than has

been recognized, and may feel a need to search for their biological parents.

Colon (1978), an adoptee, writes that a child's experience of biological-familial continuity and connection is a basic ingredient in his or her sense of self, personal significance, and identity. People who experience unresolved emotional cut-offs from significant others are at a greater risk emotionally and psychologically than those who have resolved such cut-offs. Therefore, all adopted children should not only have good parenting, but access to information about, and perhaps eventually contact with, their biological families. However, existing adoption practices attempt to erase biological roots. Colon recommends that children should be encouraged to relate to their biological family to the extent that both parties wish. All adoptees should be given the opportunity to make a decision about this. Concerning adoptive familial connectedness versus biological-familial continuity, he concludes that individuals need to strike a realistic balance between togetherness and separateness, with freedom to move from one to the other.

Another commonly held belief is that having a good home should be enough to dispel the desire to know more about one's birthparents. However, research has shown that a desire to know one's biological roots does not spring from idle curiosity, but from genealogical concerns and questions of personal identity. In a longitudinal study, Seglow, Pringle, and Wedge (1972) compared a group of adopted children with a group of nonadopted peers in order to find answers to the following questions:

1. What kind of start do adopted children get in life?

2. Are they more at risk—at birth or later—than those in the general child population?

3. How do they fare by age seven compared to nonadopted children?

4. What do adoptive parents feel about the adopted child as he or she develops?

5. What are adoptive parents' views about their adopted child knowing his or her background, telling their child of adoption, and about the adoption process in general?

They concluded that adoptive parents must understand that their child will want to know of the adoption and background information about their biological parents. A lack of this background information may result in the child experiencing "genealogical bewilderment." Dr. Betty Allen, a psychologist and an adoptee, has stated that it may be almost impossible to understand fully the intensity of this need without having experienced, firsthand, the frustration of knowing that information exists, but is unavailable to those it most deeply affects (Morrison, 1983).

In 1973, Triseliotis interviewed 70 adoptees (29 male, 41 female) who had sought information about their backgrounds. He found that adoptees strongly resented it if they learned of their adoption from outside sources and were bitter toward parents who were reluctant to tell them. Adoptees who were given little or no background information or who received information related in a hostile way generally were intent on finding birthparents. Those who were told something positive about their natural parents were inclined to search for additional information on their genealogical background. Also, those satisfied with their adoptive home life were looking mainly for the information that would help them to have a better understanding of themselves. Those who were dissatisfied were looking for nurturing from a parent. Factors related to bringing about a search included: nondisclosure or hostile revelation of background genealogical information, poor home relationships, negative self-esteem, and having had psychiatric help.

Four years later, Pannor and Nerlove (1977), after conducting an eight-week counseling session for adoptive parents and adoptive adolescents, found that adoptive parents were still anxious because of their children's interest in their backgrounds, and that the adolescents sensed that their curiosity would embarrass or threaten their parents. The teenagers most frequently wanted to know, "Why do people give children up for adoption?" Out of the 13 adolescents, ages 12–19, only two said that they were satisfied with the adoption information given them by their parents.

Research examining the characteristics of adult adoptees who contact agencies or search groups to find their birthparents has found that most of these adoptees had very limited knowledge of their backgrounds (Kowal & Schilling, 1985). Conclusions from a study exploring the reasons 100 adult adoptees pursued searches for their birthparents revealed that most adoptees were either motivated by the desire to resolve confusion or by a sense of emptiness. In the second largest group, adoptees mentioned a strong desire for further self-understanding. Self-understanding reflected their wishes for further knowledge about physical features and personality development. The third largest group of adoptees sought their birthparents for pragmatic reasons, such as medical information. Most members of this group emphasized that they had enjoyed their childhoods and identified their adoptive parents as their "true" parents. In contrast, the fourth group searched directly for a sense of belonging, often resulting from strained relationships with adoptive parents or the death of an adoptive parent in childhood. This fourth group included only 15 percent of the total sample.

These results indicate that most searches are predicated upon a lack of needed information. Information most desired by adoptees included their parents' medical histories, personality characteristics, physical descriptions, names, and ethnic backgrounds. Over half the sample also desired knowledge of their own early medical history, the reason they were placed for adoption, and their birthparents' personal interests, occupations, educations, and marital status.

The subjects reported that they received minimal information about their medical and social histories. Such lack of disclosure may be traced to sealed records in adoption agencies or to the failure of adoptive parents to tell adoptees about their backgrounds. Adoptees may have also forgotten information that was provided to them when they were children. Adoptees who have been given complete information about their birthparents are less likely to feel compelled to pursue a search. However, evidence that feelings of confusion and emptiness were the strongest motivating factors for adult adoptees to find their birthparents lends strength to the arguments espoused by advocates of open adoption. The authors suggested that the sharing of information that occurs in open and semiopen forms of adoption may alleviate the doubt that leads to the negative feelings and sense of incompleteness described by the adult adoptees.

Adoptees also search for more background information out of fear of committing incest. In recent years, there have been several documented cases of unwitting incest, including a son who unknowingly married his mother and a brother who married his half-sister. In 1960, Israel passed an open-records law primarily to avert such disasters (Morrison, 1983).

In addition, it is often critical for adoptees to have their extensive medical histories because many diseases are genetically transmitted or manifest themselves long after a birthparent has made an adoption plan for a child. While agencies generally recognize the adoptees' need for such information, their records are sometimes incomplete and/or inaccurate. Thus, adoptees are left with little medical information unless birthparents have continued to update their files (Pannor, 1985).

An open-records law would enable adoptees to know their birthparents' identities. However, opponents of such a law have estimated that 5 percent or less of the adoptees in this country want to know their birthparents' identities. For example, fewer than 1 percent of the 14,000 adoptees placed through the Edna Gladney Maternity Home in Fort Worth, Texas, have initiated a search (Foster, 1979). Proponents estimate that 10 to 20 percent are searching for their birthparents (Small, 1979: Zeilinger, 1979).

The idea that adult adoptees should, as a matter of right, have access to their birth records dates back to 1971 with the founding of the Adoptees' Liberty Movement Association (ALMA). There are now over 60 chapters of the organization. Since its founding by Florence Anna Fisher, more than a million adult adoptees have connected with their birthparents, and approximately 700,000 are on their registry for possible matching.* ALMA also leads active state-by-state campaigns for an open-records law (Cliff, 1983; Sachdev, 1984).

*Florence Anna Fisher, 1987: personal communication.

ALMA justifies its support of open adoption records by the following:

1. It is an affront to human dignity and civil rights to be denied access to one's birth records (Morrison, 1983; Sachdev, 1984).
2. Adoptees are victims of an "adoption game" in which they are forced to believe their birthparents are insignificant or dead and that their adoptive parents are their real parents (Sachdev, 1984).
3. Adult nonadoptees are not required to obtain a court order to gain access to their birth records (Zeilinger, 1979).
4. Nonadoptees do not have falsified birth certificates and are not exposed to potential medical problems and incest as a result of lack of knowledge (Foster, 1979; Morrison, 1983).
5. Once adoptees reach adulthood, it is not necessary to protect them under an agreement that was entered into on their behalf when they were children (Small, 1979).

Proponents such as Joanne Small (1979), founder of Adoptees in Search, believe that the 5 million adoptees in the United States are victims of discrimination. She points out that, as a minority group, adoptees are not as highly visible as Blacks or Hispanics and that it is their status, not ethnicity, that sets them apart. She states that adult adoptees who search are labeled as lacking impulse control and that these adults remain forever children in terms of adoption law and practice.

Laurie Flynn (1979), past president of the North American Council on Adoptable Children (NACAC) and adoptive mother, urges all adoptive parents to recognize that their children's identities involve having two sets of parents. Thus, it can be very unsettling to the whole family when the adopted child begins to deal with this fact and perhaps even wants to search for his or her birthparents. She says it is the role of adoptive parents to tolerate and even encourage this kind of curiosity. By providing love and open communication, they can strengthen their parent/child relationships.

However, there are many critics of an open-records law. The main arguments presented are that an open-records law would: (a) help to unravel the adoptive family unit by shifting the focus away from the adoptive family to a preoccupation with biological family members (Broadhurst & Schwartz, 1979; Harrington, 1979); (b) enhance and transform into reality the adoptive parents' fear that they might lose their children (Geissinger, 1984; Zeilinger, 1979); (c) lead to a totally open adoption system where children would be raised by their adoptive parents, but have frequent visits by birthparents (Foster, 1979; Pierce, 1983); (d) increase birthparent reluctance to make adoption plans for their children, with a resultant sharp decline in adoption and a corresponding rise in abortion rates (Foster, 1979; Morrison, 1983).

The aforesaid opinions are supported by the courts. One survey (Harrington, 1979) of legislative action in the 50 states showed that the policies of anonymity for birthparents and the confidentiality of court adoption proceedings have not been abandoned. In most states, a court order is still required for adult adoptees to obtain identifying information about their birthparents (NCFA, 1985).

Thus, the idea that confidentiality in adoption protects members of the adoption triad from emotional trauma continues to prevail even though there is almost a total lack of research on the issues involved. Austin Foster (1979), a clinical director and consulting psychologist for the Edna Gladney Maternity Home, points out that few people realize that sealed records are peculiar to U.S. law. There is no basis in Roman law in which adoption was primarily thought of as honorific. In most Western countries (England, Scotland, France, Finland, etc.) adoption is thought of as a charitable act in which a benevolent family decides to rear a child in need. In the United States, however, adoption is based on the assumption that the adopted child is to become, both in law and in fact, a complete member of the family, with exactly the same rights given to a natural child. Foster believes that this is why the United States has the most successful adoption system in the world, and that to tamper with this system would be disastrous. He feels that open records would be traumatic and disruptive to the parent-child relationship, that this practice would promote confusion and ambiguity for the adopted child, and would increase feelings of guilt in birthparents.

Paul Sachdev (1984), a professor at the School of Social Work, Memorial University of Newfoundland, and one of the few research specialists in adoption, describes this confidentiality in adoption as a promoter of an "as if" concept. Adoptive parents can believe adoptees never belonged to any other parents and belong to them "as if" they were of their own blood. The birthmother can pretend "as if" she never had a child. Adoptees can identify with their adoptive parents "as if" they were their real parents.

In one of the few studies thus far on adoptive parents' attitudes on open birth records, Geissinger (1984) found that a majority of the adoptive parents supported a measure allowing adult adoptees access to birth records, if agreeable to birthparents and adoptive parents. Of the 42 adoptive fathers and mothers surveyed, 45 percent agreed that adoptees should have access to birth records upon reaching age 21; and 40.5 percent thought they should have access only if agreeable to the birthparents. The most influential factor in parents' attitudes was their fear of loss and rejection. As the children grew older, this fear of rejection became strongly associated with parental position on open records. However, 97.6 percent of the parents felt that no access was totally unacceptable. Geissinger concluded that there is a growing willingness to be open and that confidentiality can no longer be guaranteed.

Finally, DiGiulio (1987), also studying adoptive-parent attitudes toward opening sealed records, found that the manner in which adoptive parents resolve their role conflict about being adoptive parents influences their attitudes about opening records. Adoptive parents who acknowledge the difference between birth and adoptive parenthood were more inclined toward opening records.

Also limited is the research on birthparents' feelings about relinquishment (Rynearson, 1982) and reunions (Silber & Speedlin, 1982; Sorosky et al., 1978) and their right to privacy (Sanders & Sitterly, 1981). Only recently have birthparents moved from being considered providers of babies to clients in their own right. The prevailing attitudes have been that birthparents will forget about an unwanted child, that birthmothers do not care about their children or they would not give them away, and that birthparents who want to know about or meet their relinquished children have not completed the mourning process (Bertocci, 1978; Silber & Speedlin, 1982). Some suggest (Bertocci, 1978; Watson, 1979) that agencies have been speaking for birthparents whom they barely and briefly knew many years ago. It is a possibility that some birthparents may no longer wish to maintain the anonymity they were promised.

Deykin, Campbell, and Patti (1984) found that the experience of placing a child through a confidential adoption had a negative impact on birthmothers' subsequent marital relationships. Some birthmothers showed both a decrease in self-esteem (feeling unfit to become a mother again) and an over-idealization of the child for whom they had made an adoption plan. For example, some did not want to have another child because it would be unfaithful to the first child. Society's growing acceptance of children born to unmarried mothers may serve to increase the unresolved feelings of birthmothers who surrendered their children years ago. The results of the study suggest that there is a need to take greater consideration of birthparents in the adoption process and to pay greater attention to their grieving and post-placement adjustment.

While it is difficult to ascertain birthparent feelings about open records, in recent years organizations such as Concerned United Birthparents, Inc. (CUB), as well as individual birthparents (Campbell, 1979) are making their feelings known. CUB has chapters in at least 25 states and publishes a national newsletter. This organization's goals are to make adoption more client-centered, to permit adult adoptees access to original birth certificates and identifying information, to allow birthparents visitation rights when adoptees are of a certain age, and to help birthparents resolve guilt feelings (Concerned United Birthparents, Inc.; Sachdev, 1984).

Nine states (California, Colorado, Florida, Louisiana, Michigan, Nevada, New York, Oregon, and Texas) have passed voluntary-consent registry laws whereby adoptees and birthparents can register their desire for contact or anonymity. Identifying information is given out only when all parties named on the original birth certificate have consented. However, critics of the registry object to it as a solution to the problem of sealed records. They (Adoptees' Liberty Movement Associations; Cliff, 1983; Campbell, 1979) feel the registry ignores the right of ownership of one's own history and makes it a matter of luck to be reunited with a birthparent.

The issues involved in the open-records debate will not fade away. Advocates will continue to press their case and feel that, in a society that values truth and openness in human dealings, an open-records system will sooner or later be recognized as a reform "whose time has come" (Zeilinger, 1979). Some suggest that adoption agencies have such a free hand to determine what confidentiality means and how state laws are interpreted, that they will play a highly significant role in providing information and reunions in the future. In fact, they will become the fourth party in adoption, making it an "adoptive rectangle" (Sachdev, 1984). Others feel that the whole issue is so complicated that, rather than an adoptive triangle of adoptive parents, birthparents, and adoptees, it should be a "pentagon" (Zeilinger, 1979), adding to the triangle the adoption agency and the courts.

2
Adoption Issues: Openness in Adoption

The debate over the need for open adoption records and the request of birthparents to have more information about their children has stimulated some agencies to revise many of their traditional adoption policies to reflect more openness in the adoption process. In 1976, Child Saving Institute of Omaha, Nebraska, implemented a new agency policy on taking pictures of the child in case birthparents, who originally chose not to see the baby in the hospital, might later wish to see what their child looked like. Their first semiopen adoption, which involved a meeting between birthparents and adoptive parents without the sharing of identifying information, occurred in 1977. This meeting resulted from the plea of a 17-year-old birthmother to meet her child's adoptive parents. Through these experiences the agency has found that open arrangements can reassure birthparents about their child's well-being and encourage the development of adoptive parents' empathy and acceptance of the birthparents. Now a wide range of options is offered, including the exchange of pictures and nonidentifying information between adoptive parents and birthparents, meetings between the two sets of parents in which either nonidentifying or identifying information could be shared, and ongoing contact between the parties involved (Sorich & Siebert, 1982). Fifty percent of their birthparents have met with adoptive parents; and thus far, there has been no negative feedback on any of these meetings from any of the parties involved (Thomas, 1985).

Meetings between birthparents and adoptive parents started in 1974 at the Children's Home Society of California (CHSC), although the agency reports that this practice has had its greatest growth in the past three years (CHSC, 1984). As of 1984, 10 percent of their adoptions could be classified as *open*, in some respects. Less than 1 percent included the exchange of last names, addresses, and phone numbers.

In 1975, Catholic Social Services of Green Bay, Wisconsin, made significant changes in their adoption program, moving from traditional adoption to open adoption (Gilling & Rauch, 1979). They noted that many adult adoptees and birthparents were approaching their agency for background information or for information about the welfare of a child who had been placed for adoption. However, their records typically lacked this kind of information. With the new conviction that an adoptee has the right to full knowledge of his or her heritage at the time of placement, all information on the child, including first and last names of birthparents, are given to adoptive parents. Birthparents write autobiographies and provide photographs of themselves and their families, knowing full well that their child will have access to them.

Catholic Social Services of Green Bay also offers meetings between birthparents and adoptive parents (Gilling & Rauch, 1979). Meetings take place either before the birth of the child, at the time of placement, or after placement of the child. Without exception, the parties involved have reported favorable feelings. Birthparents have said they gain a more realistic picture of their child's future and the type of home he or she will be reared in and feel more a part of the placement process. The agency believes that adoptive parents develop an increased awareness and appreciation of the birthparents' circumstances by such a meeting and that, should the child wish to seek out his or her birthparents, the adoptive parents will have more understanding of how that child might be received by them.

In the summer of 1981, the San Antonio and Corpus Christi regional offices of Lutheran Social Service of Texas (LSST) began to offer prospective adoptive parents and birthparents the option of face-to-face meetings (Kelly, 1984; Lutheran Social Service of Texas, Inc., 1982). Other LSST offices have begun to follow suit. In the beginning, these meetings were held at the LSST offices and could occur before or after the placement of a child. Sometimes the child is included in the first meeting (at placement), but never before the two sets of parents first have had a chance to talk (Kelly, 1984). In some cases, both sets of parents have even elected to maintain contact without the agency's direct participation.

Adoptive parents and birthparents have reported very positive feelings about these meetings. Both parties say they see each other as real people and thus do not fantasize about each others' qualities or attributes. The LSST staff believes that birthparents seem more quickly to handle their grief over not being able to parent their child. They also feel that the adopted child will be the main beneficiary of such meetings by having ready access to typical questions, such as "Who do I look like?" and "Why was I adopted?" (Cordes, 1983; Forest, 1983; Kelly, 1984).

Since the late 1970s, many other adoptive agencies and independent services in the United States have begun offering some open options. The following are among the growing number of agencies offering openness: Boys and Girls Aid Society of Portland; Open Adoptive and Family Services in Eugene, Oregon; Adoption Option in Denver; Community Family and Children Services in Traverse City, Michigan; Catholic Social Services of Helena, Montana; Options for Pregnancy in Seattle; Medina Children's Home in Seattle; Methodist Mission in San Antonio, Texas; and Children's Home Society of Minnesota. Jeanne Lindsay (1987) identified several new independent adoption services in California that offer open options for birthparents and adoptive parents. The Independent Adoption Center, which started in 1983 in Pleasant Hill, Calvary Chappel, which opened in 1979 in Downey, and New Beginnings, which was begun in 1983 in Santa Ana, are among the programs designed to promote contact between birth and adoptive families.

In 1985, Rillera and Kaplan published a handbook for planning an adoption in which there is ongoing contact between birthparents and adoptive parents. It is based on the perspective that adopted children should have access to both birth and adoptive families and "should be given progressive participation in decisions which affect his/her life" (p. 1). In such an adoptive relationship, birthparents are involved in the child's life, not to assume the role of parents, but the role of special friend or Aunt or Uncle.

Although there are many independent programs advocating full disclosure, most agencies appear to be primarily involved in promoting the sharing of information between adoptive and birthparents. It is estimated that about 35 percent of agencies also assist families in arranging face-to-face meetings, and only about 70 percent have families who participate in fully disclosed adoptions (Belbas, 1987).

There is a growing controversy over openness in the adoptions practice for two main reasons. First, there is no consensus among adoption professionals as to what openness or open placement means. Second, the practice of open placement is relatively new and its impact on members of the adoptive triad—birthparents, adoptive parents, and adopted children—has not been adequately addressed by research. In this section, definitions of openness will be presented, along with a discussion of the benefits and risks involved in changing traditional adoption practice.

In their letter of April 15, 1981, the Ad Hoc Committee to Reevaluate Adoptive Placement Philosophy, a nationwide committee formed to examine adoption policies, defined open placement in the following way (as cited by Catholic Social Services, 1983):

> Open Placement recognizes that adoption is a lifelong process involving the adoptee, birthparents, and adoptive parents. Open placement affirms that an adoptee, although relinquished and

a full member of his/her adoptive family, nevertheless remains connected to his/her birthfamily. Although legal and nurturing rights are transferred from birthparents to adoptive parents, both sets of parents recognize the importance of keeping open avenues of communication to share valuable information during the child's minority years. Placement agencies accept the responsibility to educate and counsel both birthparents and adoptive parents for a fuller understanding of adoption as a unique institution to which both sets of parents have mutual concerns and obligations. In Open Placement, agencies will expand their services to respond sensitively to the evolving needs of all three parties to adoption.

Some agencies support this definition because they feel this degree of openness meets the needs of all the parties involved. For example, Lutheran Social Service of Texas (Silber & Speedlin, 1982) defines openness as open channels of communication between birthparents and adoptive parents. An open placement is defined as one in which birthparents and adoptive parents have a face-to-face meeting at or near the time of placement. The Children's Home Society of California (1984) defines the open-adoption option as the opportunity for some form of planned communication of an identifying nature between the adoptive family and the birthparents prior to finalization. Openness in CHSC adoptions is provided on a continuum, varying according to the needs and desires of the adoption triad. Birthparents and adopting parents either may choose to know first names only or to meet without identifying themselves, or to meet with full disclosure of names and addresses, to exchange letters, pictures, or direct phone calls. Open adoption arrangements are made only when the nature and degree of openness is mutually agreed upon.

Diane Yost, Program Director for Children's Home and Aid Society of Illinois (CHSC, 1984) says, "Openness can mean openness to hearing history about the biological family all the way through to completely open arrangements in which both families meet and have access to one another in some way throughout the years." Reuben Pannor (Pannor & Baran, 1984; CHSC, 1984), former Director of Community Services, Vista Del Mar Child-Care Service, Los Angeles, California, says,

"Open adoption begins with a meeting between the birthparents and the adoptive parents. Beyond that there needs to be some arrangement worked out between birthparents and the adoptive family so that there is continued communication between them." He believes that adoption truly means incorporating another set of parents into the family's life.

Others, such as William L. Pierce, President of the National Committee for Adoption (CHSC, 1984), define open adoption as the exchange of identifying information. A more restricted view of open adoption is expressed by Ruby Lee Piester, Director of Development and former Executive Director of the Edna Gladney Maternity Home (CHSC, 1984). She says, "when I say open, I'm saying to share with the child why a mother would place the child for adoption." In contrast, Carole Anderson, incoming President of Concerned United Birthparents, Inc. (CUB) says, "adoption without full exchange of information can only be called semi-open" (CHSC, 1984).

The growing trend toward more openness in adoption practice stems not only from the belief that, in independent adoptions, the birthparents have the right to choose those who will raise their children (Baran, Pannor, & Sorosky, 1976), but also from the belief that school-aged or older children cannot be asked to sever their relationships with their biological families or other meaningful persons (Borgman, 1982; Jewett, 1978). Borgman (1982) suggests that openness demands more from an adoptive family, and that, for it to work, the openness must be structured. The family must also be willing either to adhere to the agreed-upon structure or to change it.

In 1976, Baran, Pannor, and Sorosky began to advocate an open-adoption policy that would meet the needs of some children who had not been placed for adoption. Through their work with birthparents, they found that many young women chose to keep their babies because of agency practice in a "closed system with sealed records." The women felt they were being asked to give up and to pretend that their children had died. Yet they found they could not separate themselves from a distinct part of their lives—the birth of their children.

The authors called for the offering of alternatives in adoption practice, in which birthparents could meet the adoptive parents and maintain some contact, even if minimal, with their children. In this way, birthparents could play a continual role in their children's lives. They would then have less feelings of grief, guilt, and loss and be able to build new lives for themselves. The adopted child and adoptive parents would also benefit from this contact. The children would feel less rejected, and their parents could avoid fears and fantasies and build more natural and honest relationships with their adopted children.

Some agencies have responded to this call for more openness in adoption practice by offering alternatives to confidential adoption. Sorich and Siebert (1982) state that adoption agencies are no longer mandated to maintain secrecy, mystery, and confidentiality in adoption practice. They feel that when alternatives are presented that help birthparents feel less pain and guilt, that ease adoptive parents' fears and questions, and that provide adoptees with biological continuity, the adoption process is "humanized."

Noting the decline since the early 1970s in the number of pregnant adolescents making adoption decisions, Barth (1987) reported the findings of a study to assess adolescent mothers' expectations about adoption. The majority of the 106 mothers in the sample had never considered the adoption option. The issue of uncertainty about the child's future was most influential on their decision making. Barth suggests that open practices, which encourage sharing a picture and some forms of contact, may be very appealing to pregnant adolescents.

In *Dear Birthmother,* Silber and Speedlin (1982) set forth four adoption myths that they believe can be dispelled by more openness in adoption. These are:

1. The birthmother does not care about the child or she would not give it away.

2. Secrecy in every phase of the adoption process is necessary to protect all parties.

3. Both birthparents will forget about an unwanted child.

4. If adoptees really loved their families, they would not have to search for birthparents.

They assert that adoptive parents must realize that they can never totally parent their child because they cannot give them their biological heritage or genetic future. Furthermore, adoption is a lifelong experience in which there is much need for open and honest communication between members of the adoption triad. Openness and open placements, while still not for everyone, can facilitate this kind of communication and aid both sets of parents to grow secure in their roles in the adoption triad.

Pannor and Baran (1984) have created further controversy by calling for the end of all closed adoption in agency practice. They define open adoption as the process whereby birthparents and adoptive parents meet and exchange identifying information. While both sets of parents retain the right to continuing contact and access to knowledge about the child, the birthparents relinquish legal and child-rearing rights. Frequency and regularity of contact between birthparents and the adoptive family, however, is a highly individual arrangement. Pannor (1985) recently referred to open adoption as being "like a stew," or meaning different things to different people.

Based on their experience, and not on research, they conclude that open adoptions allow all parties concerned to make decisions about the kind and extent of relationship they desire. In open adoption, birthparents are full participants in the placement of their child. Thus, they are better able to cope with feelings of loss, mourning, and grief. Adoptive parents can avert fears and fallacies that negatively affect their relationship with their children. They can also give factual, firsthand background information to their child. The adoptees, through exchange of pictures, personal contacts, or letters, can gain a better understanding of their birthparents' situation and are, therefore, less likely to feel rejected by them. Through open adoption, Pannor and Baran maintain, a healthy adoption institution can be built.

There has been much criticism of open-adoption placements. Some suggest that open adoption would violate the privacy of adoptive parents and birthparents alike and would confuse the adopted child with the introduction of multiple parents (Foster, 1979; Kraft et al., 1985a,b,c; Pierce, 1983;

Zeilinger, 1979). Foster (1979) has pointed out that the *hanai* open adoption of old Hawaii is so remote from the U.S. adoption experience, where the emphasis is on individual responsibility and achievement, that the concept is not directly transferable to U.S. adoption practice.

Zeilinger (1979) argues that, legally, the agency has no right to continued contact with the parties once the adoption has been legally consummated. Ethically, he says, when adoption is considered an ongoing process, it offends social-work philosophy. Social service is a contract entered into freely by all parties with the understanding that the client can terminate the contract at any time. To prolong contact beyond this point, upon the agency's volition, is an intolerable invasion of privacy.

William Pierce (Kelly, 1984) has called openness in adoptions "very dangerous, tragic and disastrous." He enumerates the risks to the child, birthparents, and adoptive parents as follows (Pierce, 1983):

RISKS TO THE CHILD

1. A child could misinterpret information given to him leading to feelings of rejection and denial.

2. A child could question why his birthfather is not present at a meeting.

3. A child could resent an unsympathetic report of his birthparents by his adoptive parents or suspect that a sympathetic report is untrue.

RISKS TO THE BIRTHPARENT

1. In a face-to-face meeting, the birthparent(s) may feel ambivalent or may want to reject the adoptive parents but would feel uncomfortable in doing so.

2. In fairness, both birthparents should be present at the first meeting to prevent misrepresentation ("The father is a bum"). However, if one birthparent agrees to meet and the other does not the rights of the one wishing no contact could be violated.

3. At any time inconvenient or otherwise, birthparents could contact the adoptive family.

4. In California, unsupervised meetings have resulted in adoptive

parents offering gratuities to the birthmother. This leads to undue pressure or stress for the birthparent.

RISKS TO THE ADOPTIVE PARENT

1. A negative impression of a birthparent can lead to transference to the child ("You're just like your birthmom").

2. Couples who are willing to meet face-to-face will be chosen over more qualified couples who are not willing to meet.

3. Adoptive parents may worry over their dress or how best to impress the birthparents. ("What if I say something wrong, will we be rejected?")

4. Birthparents do not see adoptive parents in their "real light" when they get angry or must discipline their child.

Others, as quoted in the recent book by the Children's Home Society of California (1984), express their concern. Kirk Brown, an adoptee, a marriage and family counselor, and founder of *PACER*, a newsletter for adoptees, says that adoptive parents could buy into an open adoption too quickly out of their need to receive a child. They may agree to an open situation that, deep down inside, they might not really want. He thinks it ought to be viewed in stages and also worries about the effect on the child: "I don't think coparenting works, on the other hand, open adoption is better than closed tight adoption."

Betty Jean Lifton, an adoptee, also has reservations (Lifton, 1975):

When you're on one side with your adoptive family you have a certain security. If you have this other known family, I don't know what that does to your identity with your adoptive family. It's such a delicate balance—how much they talk about it, how much or how often they tell you. It's very hard for people to be wise psychologically when they're emotionally involved. Yet, it seems to me a healthy child would want to see those other parents.

Tony Veronico, adoptive parent and adoption professional, says she does not know about the benefits of openness to the child: "I don't know what we're providing here other than an opportunity for a biological parent to say I approve of this adoptive parent, or an adoptive parent to be able to say some day, 'I did meet your mom and dad and these are some of the reasons why.' "

Marietta Spencer, of the Children's Home Society of Minnesota, cites in her book, *The Changing Picture of Adoption,* other models of existing coparenting, such as stepparenting, stepparent adoptions, and joint custody after divorce. She writes, "It is often not a comfortable situation for the adults involved and it is often an uncomfortable one for the children. Just because it exists in our society in other areas, do we emulate it?" (Children's Home Society of California, 1984, p. 40).

Holly van Goldenwicker (1985), also of the Children's Home Society of Minnesota, suggests that open adoption may be a "quick fix" for members of the adoption triad in dealing with their feelings of loss, grief, and anger. She believes that full acceptance of the adoptive situation can only come when "distancing" occurs by the individuals involved from the object causing their angry or conflictual feelings. Since there is little distancing in an open placement, the adoptive parents, the birthparents, and the adopted child are not adequately able to express their grief or deal with their anger. They may think, "I don't have to experience grief this week, because I have a visit."

After carefully reviewing the literature and arguments for and against open adoption, Curtis (1986) concluded that longitudinal research is necessary to assess the outcomes of different adoptive arrangements. While advocates of open adoption condemn the secretive nature of closed practices, proponents of confidential adoption point to the benefits derived from greater family security and clarity of roles. In response to arguments that adoptees need knowledge of their backgrounds to develop healthy personal identities, agencies favoring more confidential adoption assert that such information may be derived through greater access to records, not by personal contact between adoptees and their natural parents. Existing research is especially inconsistent in regard to the effects of open adoption on the birthmother and the necessity of her grieving process. According to proponents of open adoption, knowledge of her child's well-being helps the birthmother work through her loss because she is not troubled by uncertainty. Advocates of confidential adoption contend that closed adoption allows a greater resolution of the grieving process because it precludes unrealistic fantasies of reunion. Curtis believes that current theories are based on highly abstract philosophical ideals that are not grounded in actual experience. In order to provide some credibility and validity to discussions of open adoption, longitudinal research must be completed to determine and compare the outcomes of differing adoption practices.

Currently it appears that open adoption may produce extremely satisfying relationships for adoptive parents and birthparents who mutually agree to have ongoing contact. When either party is unwilling to participate in an open arrangement, a different match between adoptive parents and birthparents should be considered.

From the preceding discussion, it can be clearly seen that there are a number of opinions, not based on research, as to the merits of open adoption. Besides the study reported in this book, only one research study on openness has been published to date. Belbas (1987) conducted a small exploratory study involving 12 families who had experienced differing degrees of openness. She found that all parents "felt unprepared by previous life events for the unique experiences and feelings of open adoption." All parents were found to be empathic toward their child's biological parent and toward how the child might feel about being adopted. All adoptive parents also described "emotional knowing," or feeling and thinking about the experience from the perspective of the biological parent. Most responses to birthparents were thoughtful and nonjudgmental.

Three concerns in reference to open adoptions emerged. First, in families with more than one adopted child, concern was expressed for the child who did not have ongoing contact with his or her birthparents. Second, concern was expressed that the birthparents would disappear from the child's life. Third, concern about helping the maturing child understand the role of the birthmother in his or her life was noted.

Most adoptive parents indicated that openness affected their everyday lives. They felt closer to the child and noted complications similar to divorce, where there are parents and step-parents. Openness is a constant reminder that they are not the child's only parents.

Other than the Belbas (1987) study there is no research literature in existence on which to base a change in current adoption policy. The consequences of open adoption for the parties involved have not been documented. Only recently (Kraft et al., 1985a, 1985b, 1985c) have major psychological issues been raised concerning the effects of open adoption on birthmothers, adoptive parents, and adopted children. These psychological issues seem to be the only ones presented in the literature and will be discussed here in detail.

Issues formulated about birthparents are based on work with adolescent females who have decided to carry their pregnancies to term. The authors note that adolescence is the time when the sense of self is developing. Therefore, a pregnant teenager still may have many unresolved feelings about herself, her parents, and about parenting her child. Thus, she is faced with developmental tasks and decisions far beyond her years.

Another issue is that adolescents' cognitive levels vacillate between child and adult levels of functioning. Thus pregnancy can be viewed as a vague and unreal possibility, and when it occurs, it can be viewed as a means of achieving closeness and intimacy. Thus, many pregnant teenagers are not cognitively or emotionally capable of assessing the consequences of a decision to relinquish and maintain contact. In fact, they may be confused by the mixed messages of "terminate your rights, but also maintain contact with the adoptive parents and child."

The adolescent's unconscious needs, which lead to her pregnancy, can continue after the adoption is finalized. In other words, the meaning of the child to the birthmother will determine the relationship the birthmother will fantasize having with the child. These needs may interfere with adoptive parenting in the sense that the birthmother may have competitive feelings about the parents who adopted her child. She may have conflictual feelings involving envy and jealousy as she sees the child grow—reachable but unattainable. At some point, birthmothers also must begin to face the loss and pain involved in making an adoption plan for their child. Grief and mourning enable them to put the experience into perspective. However, in open adoptions, they cannot experience loss; at best, something is given in exchange for hoped-for relief. In addition, birthparents sometimes may be searching for a new and more empathic set of parents in the adoptive parents. Finally, there are no cultural patterns for birthmothers to follow in open adoptions. Some may think of themselves as aunts, sisters, or godmothers, but they are placed in a difficult position of creating a model because there are no existing role models.

Kraft et al. (1985b) also believe that when open adoption is proposed, few benefits to the adoptive parents are mentioned. Adoptive parents are often given little choice and are at the mercy of agency demands if they are to achieve parenthood. Their needs and rights to privacy may be sacrificed in order to satisfy the needs of birthparents.

Several theoretical issues have been raised about adoptive parents (Kraft et al., 1985b). First, an important factor that permits comfortable attachment and bonding to the baby is security in the permanence of the relationship. When the permanence and guarantee of freedom from intrusion or interference are threatened (in reality or fantasy in an open adoption), anxieties will arise, which are disruptive to the parent-child relationship and to the adopted infant's development. Whatever the contact, through letters, meetings, pictures, or gifts, the adoptive parents' sense of security may be threatened when the contact stimulates and reinforces conscious or unconscious fears of loss of their baby. Second, adoptive parents' ability to form and maintain a healthy, ongoing parent-child bond are affected by feelings about the adoptive infant and birthmother. They may feel guilty about receiving benefits from the birthmother's misfortune or pain. Third, the task of dealing with feelings about infertility and the adoption become more difficult for adoptive parents when there is continued contact. Conflictual feelings of worthlessness and guilt about infertility may become reactivated when there is continued contact. The adoptive parents must deal with resentments all parents feel when their authority is questioned, while also handling feelings of helplessness and confusion, as their children inevitably react to and challenge two sets of parental figures. The authors believe it is difficult enough to raise biological children; adoptive parenting is made even more complex by introducing openness factors which may interfere with adoptive parenting in a "serious and subtle" way.

In the third paper, the authors (Kraft et al., 1985c) discuss the adopted child's psychological development through infancy, oedipal, latency, and adolescence stages and contend that open adoption in each of these developmental stages interferes with the child's need to internalize one set of parents. Potential risks noted to the adopted child in infancy are that, during infancy, the parent-child bond can be affected by any form of contact between the adoptive parents and birthparents; by the adoptive mother's guilt feelings over her involvement with the birthmother; and by the adoptive parents' need to be supportive of the birthmother. During the oedipal phase of development, having to maintain a relationship with two sets of parents can be extremely confusing to the adopted preschooler. During the latency phase, having access to or knowing the birthparent will not lessen an adopted child's vulnerability to fantasy, because all children are "great myth-makers." In addition, the knowledge of being adopted can be very important to a latency-aged child's sense of belonging. In an open adoption, the result may be a feeling on the part of all concerned that the adoption is closer to a foster placement than an adoption. The main developmental task of adolescents is to separate emotionally from their psychological parents and to develop a strong sense of self. The adolescents' feelings toward their parents at this time are often confused, volatile, and mercurial. Open adoptions would invite an acting out of this developmental ambivalence toward their adoptive parents.

In their summary of the three papers, the authors acknowledge that neither open nor closed adoptions offer perfect solutions to the parties involved. In other words, what is best for the birthparent may be damaging to the child or what is best for the adoptive parents may be problematic for the birthmother. They conclude, however, that the consequences of open adoption on the adoption triad must be carefully considered before there can be drastic policy changes and that some of the issues they have raised can only be answered by more research.

To demonstrate the advantages of open adoption, Ryburn (1987) addresses historical reasons for the practice of confidential adoption that are no longer relevant or desirable in today's society. The traditional emphasis on a monogamous family (Engels, 1972), which produced children of "undisputed paternity," allowed little recognition of an adopted child's birthparents. Such a narrow view of kinship is not conducive to open forms of adoption, which provide the child contact with both birthparents and his or her adoptive parents. Confidential adoption also served to alleviate the stigma attached to an adopted child because of presumed illegitimacy. By not knowing the possibly "immoral" details of his or her background, confidential adoption protected the child. Confidential adoption additionally could protect the adoptive parents by presumably allowing them to create better bonding and maintain a primary attachment to the child. Historically, the importance of blood kinship in regard to inheritance has also served to continue confidential forms of adoption. Legally, confidential adoptions reinforced the adoptive parents' claim to the child and guaranteed the adopted child's right to their estate, free from entanglements with birthparents.

Ryburn (1987) points to several ideological assumptions that accompany confidential adoptions. Confidential adoptions are based on a belief in substitutability; that adoptive parents may unequivocally substitute for birthparents. Likewise, the child's knowledge of his or her genetic and social background is viewed as inconsequential in developing a solid sense of personal identity. Though confidential adoption was historically preferable for economic and social reasons, changing values have made the practice less desirable. Current attention to the importance of personal identity and the freedom of choice in family lifestyles and relationships has created the need for the option for open adoption.

Open adoption emphasizes voluntary arrangements, based on goodwill, which are subject to ongoing negotiation and change. Since the parties involved in the adoption are responsible for decisions made, they will inevitably feel greater control in the adoption process. The primary client in open adoption should always be the child. Open adoption allows the child to gain information about his social, medical, and genealogical history, understanding of developmental features such as personality, and an explanation of why he or she was placed for adoption. Benefits to adoptive parents include a confirmation of their role as acting parents and freedom from uncertainty about their child's birthparents. Birthparents gain control and satisfaction in their ability to choose adoptive parents and develop an identification with them. This identification allows a more complete, resolved grieving process. Ryburn's observations of these advantages are largely taken from interviews with families who have experienced both open and confidential adoptions in New Zealand. While the agency has facilitated contact between adoptive parents and birthparents, adoptive parents have found much greater satisfaction in arrangements that allow them to have very significant choices in adoption-related decisions.

In conclusion, the open-adoption records and openness in adoption practice controversies will continue to be debated in the absence of scientific research. There has been some research on adoptees' need for background information (Seglow, Pringle, & Wedge, 1972; Sorosky, Baron, & Pannor, 1975; Triseliotis, 1973), but very little documentation on birthparent feelings (Rynearson, 1982; Silber & Speedlin, 1982), adoptive parent feelings (Geissinger, 1984), and adoptees' feelings (Lifton, 1979) toward openness in adoption. As Watson (1979) has said, there are no absolute answers to the adoption issues of today. With a solution to one problem, new problems are generated and must be solved; it is a never-ending process. Because of this great need for research, the study to be reported in this book was designed to assess the impact of differing degrees of openness on adoptive parents and corresponding birthparents.

3
Theoretical Perspectives on Openness

Although there is currently no comprehensive or accepted theory of adoptive family relationships, a number of other theories suggest implications or raise questions concerning the practice of openness in adoption. This section provides a brief overview of the main features and issues raised by attachment theory, goodness-of-fit theory, cognitive developmental theory, cognitive dissonance theory, family systems theory, and Kirk's adoptive kinship theory.

ATTACHMENT THEORY

Attachment theory has its roots in ethological theory (Bowlby, 1969; Ainsworth, 1973) and holds that the primary function of the attachment relationship is to ensure the proximity of the immature infant to its caregiver for provision of safety and food. The infant's behaviors, such as crying, cooing, babbling, smiling, and following serve to bring the infant into close contact with the caregiver. Recent versions of attachment theory emphasize not only the goal of proximity maintenance, but also the goal of achieving "felt security" through the relationship (Sroufe & Waters, 1977).

When placed in an assessment situation that involves multiple episodes of the caregiver's entering and leaving a room (the "Strange Situation," Ainsworth, 1979), "securely" attached infants explored a novel environment freely in their mother's presence. They did not necessarily cry when their mothers left the room, but they did greet their return with pleasure. In contrast, "avoidant" babies avoided contact with their mothers upon reunion, sometimes actively looking away and averting their gaze. Distress was as easily comforted by a stranger as by the mother. "Resistant" or "ambivalent" babies were quite distressed when their mothers left, but were difficult to console upon reunion. They often resisted contact with their mothers, while at the same time signaling that they wanted to be comforted.

Focused attachment relationships such as those just described develop gradually over the first year of life. According to Ainsworth and colleagues, the roots of secure attachment lie in the caregiver's responsiveness to the needs of the infant. In a feeding situation, mothers of securely attached infants have been found to be more sensitive, accepting, and psychologically accessible than mothers of anxiously attached infants (Ainsworth et al., 1978). Mothers of avoidant infants seemed to be especially rejecting and had an aversion to physical contact. Recent evidence (Egeland & Farber, 1984) suggests that some resistant babies may be more difficult to care for early in life (e.g., they may be less alert or active than other babies). When coupled with caregivers who were not unusually sensitive, the attachment relationships may have taken this distinctive turn.

A sizable body of evidence has accrued to date to indicate that attachment relationships in infancy have long-term consequences for the psychological and relational functioning of the individual child. For example, toddlers who were more securely attached as infants have been shown to be more willing to explore a novel physical environment than are toddlers who were anxiously attached infants (Hazen & Durrett, 1982). In addition, securely attached infants showed better problem-solving ability and sociability at age two (Matas, Arend, & Sroufe, 1978; Pastor, 1981), and more curiosity and flexibility during the preschool years (Arend, Gove, & Sroufe, 1979), than did their anxiously-attached peers. These and other studies suggest a great deal of continuity in the legacy of attachment from infancy through early childhood.

Because of attachment theory's emphasis on the caregiver's sensitivity and psychological accessibility to the infant, one might predict that openness in adoption could jeopardize the development of this relationship (Kraft et al., 1985b). If the adoptive parents' sense of security is threatened by contact with birthparent(s), the quality of parenting behavior might be negatively affected by making it difficult for the adoptive parents to interact wholeheartedly with the infant. Another possible reaction would be for the adoptive parents to over-compensate and become hypervigilant or intrusive in their parenting. To the degree that agencies suggest that adoptive parents owe something to birthparents, this may engender feelings of guilt, which could in turn complicate the development of attachment. In addition, if the adoptive parents feel that they are expected to provide emotional support for the birthmother, this may take their focus away from the baby and detract from their task of developing a sense of attachment with the infant (Kraft et al., 1985c). Conversely, if adoptive parents know the birthmother and know that they do not have to worry about her trying to reclaim the baby, they can relax and be more attentive parents; attachment may be enhanced.

GOODNESS-OF-FIT THEORY

Goodness-of-fit theories hold that an individual's development is optimized in those situations where there is an optimal "match" or "fit" between characteristics of the individual and characteristics or demands of the environment in which the individual functions. Examples of this model include: J. McVicker Hunt's (1961) "notion of the match" in intellectual development; Holland's (1973, 1985) concept of person-environment congruency in the occupational world; and Lerner's (1985) goodness-of-fit model of infant temperament and environmental responsiveness. Consistent with attachment theory, goodness-of-fit theory states that, when infants are raised by parents who understand them and are sensitive to their needs, development will be optimized. When parents are not able to accommodate the needs of their children, mismatch problems may occur.

Such problems may occur with greater frequency in adoptive than in biological families, since adoptive parents are less similar to their children in several ways, on average. Data from studies of family similarities (e.g., Horn, 1983; Scarr & Weinberg, 1983) suggest that, for IQ, the average parent-child correlation in biological families is approximately .40; whereas, in adoptive families it is approximately .14, even though the adopted child has lived with his or her adoptive parents from early infancy into middle adolescence. For personality, average correlations are approximately .15 for biological parent-child pairs and .07 for adoptive parent-child pairs. In addition, adoptive parents are typically highly educated, of middle to upper middle socioeconomic status, and are married longer when they first become parents (through adoption) than are unselected biological parents, whose children reside with them (e.g., Zill, 1985).

From results such as these, one could predict that the degree of actual and perceived similarity would be less in adoptive than in biological families. Mismatches may occur between intellectual levels or personalities of parents and children, between characteristics of adopted siblings, or between adopted children and biological children within the same family. When major mismatches occur, the stage may be set for conflict or for parental disappointment. Therefore, on the basis of goodness-of-fit theory, it is predicted that the incidence of problems would be higher in adoptive than in biological families. Furthermore, it is predicted that the magnitude of the discrepancy will be positively correlated with the likelihood of problems.

In earlier work concerning adopted adolescents in residential treatment for emotional disorders, we found that the perception of incompatibility was greatest in adoptive families in which parents either accentuated or diminished the importance of the child's heredity (Grotevant, McRoy, & Jenkins, in press). When the importance of heredity was accentuated, parents attributed their adopted adolescents' problem behavior to biology, abdicating any responsibility for their own role in creating or ameliorating the problem. When the importance of heredity was diminished, parents appeared to deny the difference between adoptive and biological parenting, which then put them at risk for problematic communication about adoption with their adolescents (Kirk, 1981). A more adaptive position appears to be one that acknowledges the joint role of the child's heredity and parenting behavior in the child's socialization.

Goodness-of-fit theory suggests that matching of adoptive parents and birthparents might be especially important in cases involving open adoptions. A child's feeling of being "different" from the adoptive family might be exacerbated by the feeling that he or she has more in common with the birthparents. Such a situation might undermine the adoptive parents' ability to fulfill their role as parents and might add confusion to the adolescent's developing sense of self.

COGNITIVE-DEVELOPMENTAL THEORY

In recent research, Brodzinsky, Singer, and Braff (1984) documented clear developmental changes in children's understanding of the meaning of adoption. In keeping with the cognitive-developmental tradition, they suggested that the child's understanding of adoption is a constructive process that does not reach a mature level until adolescence.

Although adoptive parents may begin talking with their child at an early age about adoption, it will be necessary for ongoing discussion to take place in order to help the child develop a mature concept of the meaning of adoption. In terms of cognitive-developmental theory, then, the timing and content of adoption revelation will have a major impact on the child's developing concept of adoption, as well as on the child's concept of self-as-adopted-child.

Brodzinsky, Singer, and Braff (1984) suggested that many adoptive parents overestimate their child's understanding of their adoption and therefore may stop talking about it before the child has a mature concept. Their results imply that information about adoption must be developmentally matched to the child's ability to understand it, and that repeated discussions of the meaning of adoption must take place over time, especially into early adolescence.

From the perspective of open adoptions, cognitive-developmental theory suggests that having information about one's birthparents or having a personal relationship with them might facilitate the child's understanding of his or her own identity. On the other hand, it means that the child's task is more complex because the child has to construct his or her understanding of the birthparents, the relationship to the birthparents, and his or her own adoptive status. There is currently no information in the literature on this process.

Cognitive-developmental theory also suggests that the child's understanding needs to be "updated" periodically. Adoptive parents whose children have ongoing relationships with birthparents will need to ascertain the way in which the child understands that relationship and work with the child toward facilitating this understanding at a level the child can comprehend.

COGNITIVE DISSONANCE THEORY

Cognitive dissonance theory, developed by Festinger (1957), is concerned with the relations among cognitions. Two cognitions are consonant if one cognition follows from or "fits" with the other, and dissonant if one cognition is discrepant from or follows from the opposite of the other. When a person discovers dissonant cognitions, tension is created and he or she is driven to reduce this resulting unpleasant state. Dissonance may be reduced by either changing cognitions, adding cognitions, or altering the importance of cognitions.

Prior to making decisions, people are thought to be receptive to all information in an attempt to make the most rational decision possible (Festinger, 1964). However, once a decision has been made, dissonance-reducing processes begin. People will seek out information that confirms the wisdom of their decision, ignore or reduce the importance of information that runs contrary to their decision, and will see the chosen alternative as increasingly attractive, while judging the nonchosen alternative as increasingly unattractive.

With respect to open adoptions, cognitive dissonance theory addresses the vulnerability of prospective adoptive parents to the recommendations of agency personnel concerning openness. Even if a parent is opposed to openness in principle, his or her desire to adopt may be so strong as to overpower any objections to an open adoption. Parents may feel that if saying "yes" to an open adoption is what it will take to get a child, then they will agree to an open adoption. This situation creates dissonance—agreeing to go along with a practice that is actually disagreeable. Once the decision to participate in an open adoption is made, the parents will then engage in dissonance-reducing behaviors. The reluctant parents may seek out information that confirms their point of view and become the most vocal advocates of openness.

Discrepant cognitions may also arise when the adopted child begins to understand that being adopted means that he or she was "relinquished," or "given up," or "given away" by birthparents. This understanding may contribute to the child's feeling of unworthiness or of being a rejectable person and may contrast sharply with messages of caring from the adoptive parents. In order to resolve these discrepancies, or reduce the tension of these dissonant cognitions, the child may accentuate the negative qualities he or she is attributing to him- or herself. The child may seek out evidence to confirm that he or she is in fact unworthy of the love or care of others; may set him- or herself up to be rejected by others, thus providing evidence for his or her rejectability; or may also diminish the importance of the messages of support or love he or she is receiving from others. Another approach to reducing the dissonance is to denigrate the birthparents, a solution which may result in unhealthy feelings of hostility.

Even though birthmothers almost universally note that they chose openness so that they would make sure their children understood why they were placed for adoption, this option provides no guarantees that the child will actually understand. Open adoptions provide their share of discrepant cognitions for the child to deal with; for instance, the birthmother who has subsequent children whom she chooses to parent must surely create a set of discrepancies for the adopted child. The child will attempt to make sense of these discrepancies and resolve the situation as best he or she can.

FAMILY SYSTEMS THEORY

In family systems theory (e.g., Minuchin, 1974; Steinglass, 1987), the family is seen as a group of individuals whose behaviors reciprocally affect each other over time. The model emphasizes the importance of family organization for the functioning of the family unit and the well-being of its members. The relationships among individuals in the family are governed by boundaries, which regulate the flow of information and activity within the family. The family is organized into subsystems (e.g., husband-wife, mother-child, father-child, sibling, and others), which are differentially open (or permeable) to influence from the outside.

Family adaptation is described as the family's ability to modify its boundaries as a function of developmental change or external pressure. This type of flexibility is important to all families, but takes on special importance in the situation involving open adoption. When birthparents have ongoing, but sporadic involvement with the adoptive family, the adoptive family unit must develop a great deal of flexibility in order to adjust its boundaries as the birthparents enter and leave. When the boundaries between individuals within the family and the birthparents are unclear, the family's ability to function successfully may be impaired. This may occur, for example, when the birthparents and adoptive parents have conflicting views about the appropriate relationship between the adopted child and birthparents.

The development of flexibility requires communication, time, and energy. Such demands may add significant stress to the lives of first-time adoptive parents who are trying to accommodate the needs of their baby, while also trying to accommodate the needs and desires of the baby's birthparents. When the adoptive family has difficulty regulating this boundary, it may become inappropriately open to the birthparents (which might later engender confusion on the part of the child and others) or it might become overly rigid and cut off communication prematurely. In any case, family systems theory would predict that the adoption of a child would be a delicate time in the formation of the family and that having ongoing contact with birthparents could make the family's early adaptations quite complex.

KIRK'S ADOPTIVE KINSHIP THEORY

Kirk (1964, 1981) has applied social role theory to adoptive family relationships and suggested that adoptive parents experience a role handicap associated with their adoptive status. In other words, in contrast to biological parents, adoptive parents are put in parenting situations without the benefit of societal support. They resolve it by either acknowledging or rejecting the difference between adoptive and birth parenthood. According to Kirk, parents who are unable to acknowledge the inherent differences between adoptive and biological family situations may experience a breakdown in communication with their children about adoption concerns. According to his theory, the ideal adoptive family situation is one in which the children clearly understand the unique relationships they have with both birthparents and adoptive parents.

In open adoption, this understanding might be greatly facilitated, because the child will continually be exposed to reminders of the fact that he or she was adopted. Thus, there is no risk that the adoptive family will pretend that the child was not adopted or will deny the child access to background information. However, a vulnerability that might occur in open-adoption families could be termed "insistence of differences" (Brodzinsky, Singer, & Braff, 1984). If the child is constantly reminded of his or her adoptive status in such a way that a difference from the family is emphasized, the child may experience difficulty in feeling a full sense of belonging in the adoptive family.

Just as adoptive parents have a role handicap, birthparents can as well. The roles defined for each party are far from clear, especially during the current period in which open adoption is a relatively new concept. Therefore, Kirk's theory would predict that openness in adoption would impose strains on all parties in the adoption triad as a result of role ambiguity.

Specific predictions concerning the consequences of openness can be derived from each of the six theories discussed in this chapter. However, much of the literature on adoption is atheoretical or clinical in orientation. Future research on adoptive family relationships will be much stronger if it is theory-driven.

4
Agency Practices

In order to glean further information on various agency attitudes and practices concerning open adoptions, the authors interviewed the professional counseling staff at The Edna Gladney Maternity Home in Forth Worth; Catholic Social Services for Montana in Helena; and the San Antonio, Corpus Christi, and Austin Regional Offices of Lutheran Social Service of Texas. In addition, through correspondence with the Catholic Social Services of Green Bay, Wisconsin, additional data were collected on their procedures and experiences with open adoptions. Information on the program at the Child Saving Institute of Omaha was obtained by telephone and at a presentation at the 1985 Minnesota Post-Legal Adoption Services Conference. Brief descriptions of each program, as well as a concluding list of summary observations, will be given. Variations will exist in some of the descriptive categories and terminology because of the different sources used for data collection.

EDNA GLADNEY MATERNITY HOME:
FORT WORTH

History

Open communication at Edna Gladney began in 1961 when the Home initiated meetings between groups of adoptive parents, unwed mothers, and adoptees. In the early 1960s, Gladney developed a "Background Folder." This folder, which was presented to the adoptive parents at the time of placement, was to be shared with their children at such time as they deemed to be appropriate. These folders were also made available to adoptees and adoptive parents when placements had occurred prior to the inception of this practice. About five years later, a group of adoptive parents, adult adoptees, and birthmothers began participating in a panel discussion at a board meeting.

Currently, although there is no actual contact between corresponding members of the adoption triad, there are opportunities for noncorresponding birthmothers, adult adoptees, and adoptive parents to meet. These meetings are designed to help biological mothers understand adoptive parents' motives for adoption and understand how adoptive parents handle the subject of adoption with adoptees. The meetings are also designed to increase empathy by helping the adoptive parents explain to their children what birthparents are like. The ultimate goal of these meetings is to establish warmth and understanding among all those involved.

Adoption Preparation Process

By the time most people apply for adoption, they have explored fertility and many are approaching their thirties. Prospective parents complete an initial information sheet and those who qualify are invited to attend an informational meeting. There they learn about the agency and tour the facility. They also talk in small groups with young women who have volunteered to meet as a panel with the adoptive applicants to discuss their feelings about Edna Gladney, adoption, and how they came to the decision to come to Gladney.

Infertility-grief work is handled in small groups. Parents are told to prepare an autobiography, which is submitted with the application. State licensing standards are met, which include office interviews and visits in the home, in addition to these autobiographical sketches. Families are encouraged to join auxiliaries, or small groups, for support and participate in an orientation to adoption. If the family does not join, the agency assumes they are not ready to adopt.

For a first-child adoption, the preparation process generally takes about four months. Individual and joint interviews are held and a home visit is made.

Most adoptive parents wish to match children with their families; and many adoptive parents desire a good medical-history background and are urged to explore with their physician any negatives, such as drugs, alcohol, or hereditary factors.

Birthmother Counseling Program

Ideally, birthmothers enter the Gladney home when they are 4–5 months pregnant, attend school there, and deliver in the campus hospital. The biological mother may visit with the baby if she so chooses. About 30 percent of the young women who enter the home decide either to leave before delivery, or to leave with the child.

Birthmothers share with the staff their personal backgrounds, both the positives and the negatives, in order to assist the agency in making the best possible plans with them for the child. They also can request certain characteristics in adoptive parents, such as religion, size of community, and good communication with their other children or with their parents. When they request it, birthmothers are able to receive a description of the family, their interests and personalities, and a description of the home.

Babies are usually placed when they are 14–16 days old. They are kept in the nursery on the campus until then. If the placement is delayed, the baby goes into one of Gladney's foster families.

Attitudes toward Openness

The agency encourages the family to prepare a scrapbook, which includes the adoption application, pictures, and other items. Gladney gives the families some standard responses they can use to tell the child about adoption. Gifts are not shared between birthparents and adoptive parents. The child is considered the gift—the gift of life. Tangible gifts are not necessary. Instead, adoptive parents are encouraged to make a general contribution to the home (e.g., toward scholarships, the building program, or other gifts), which would be for the benefit of all.

Birthparents may write letters to the child, and these are left to be shared with the child at the appropriate time. Adoptive parents sometimes write letters, and these are generally shared with the birthparents.

After the adoption, parents are encouraged to continue in the postadoptive services and are encouraged to bring their children to Edna Gladney to share information. Additionally, there is an annual Resident Reunion, and there are adult adoptee meetings. There is, in short, an involvement of the triad as they use the services of the Edna Gladney Maternity Home. According to the agency director, "the visibility of adoptive parents, and auxiliaries' contribution to the building program, have represented a positive experience for the young women."

In 1983, a voluntary registry system was established in Texas that allows adopted adults, their adult birth siblings, and birthparents to register with the Department of Human Services or their private placement agency to begin the process of attempting to establish contact between these parties. Adoptive parents are generally in favor of the Registry (TDHS, 1983), feeling that there is adequate protection for the privacy of both parties. They understand the child's natural curiosity and do not fear searching once the child is 21. Gladney educates the triad of clients about the Registry, but the law does not permit the registry of birthmothers before their infants' births. The number of registrations from either adoptees or birthparents have been relatively few. Although there was greater activity during the first year, it seems to have leveled off.

PERCEIVED RISKS OF OPEN ADOPTIONS:

—Unending contact.

—Unpredictability of people involved (no one knows what will happen in the future).

—Disruption of the child's adjustment.

—No control over the situation.

—More difficult to get closure in open adoptions (mental pictures are retained); closed adoptions provide closure for the birthmother.

—Adoptive parents and birthparents may not like each other.

—Social workers abdicate their responsibility in open adoptions.

—Gifts are an ongoing reminder and disruption in the child's life.

—Birthmothers may never separate from the child—may choose open adoption so that she does not have to separate.

—May be conflicts in extended family about contact with birthparents.

—Birthmothers seeking male acceptance may identify with the adoptive father—the adoptive mother may feel threatened.

—Girls who choose open adoptions do not really give up their children.

—May be difficult for child to understand why birthmother relinquished him or her for adoption, but kept a later-born child.

CATHOLIC SOCIAL SERVICES OF GREEN BAY, WISCONSIN

History

Operating under the auspices of the Catholic Church, Catholic Social Services has been in existence for almost 70 years. Although the agency has placed as many as 150 children a year for adoption, it currently places an average of 40. Catholic Social Services (CSS), until the late 1960s, practiced traditional adoption procedures: all identifying information was kept confidential and neither foster parents nor birthparents met adoptive parents. However, as more and more adult

adoptees and natural parents began requesting information
and questioning the agency's placement process and procedures, CSS began revising its programs. Workers began assuming undifferentiated caseloads and became equally skilled
in marriage counseling, pregnancy counseling, and adoptive
counseling. Group counseling was substituted for the original
casework approach to adoption.

Currently, all CSS adoptive parents expect and receive full
information, including identifying, on any child they receive.
Occasional meetings are held between birthparents and adoptive parents. The CSS staff are involved only in making original arrangements for these meetings. Unless asked to act as
an intermediary for future meetings, ongoing contacts between birthparents and adoptive parents are made independent of the agency.

CSS has placed over 450 children under the open concept
and report no negative experiences in any of these placements. Their adoption services include educating, advising, and
counseling natural and adoptive parents, so as to assure the
consideration of immediate and long-range needs of the child.

CSS believes that adoptive parents must recognize that
adoptive parenting is different from natural parenting. Adoptive parents must accept the reality of their infertility and the
reality of their child's natural heritage. Moreover, adoptive
parents are viewed as the adoptee's immediate and primary
source of preadoptive personal history and, thus, the vital link
in an adoptee's efforts to establish self-identity. The adoptive
parents must have the capacity to understand and accept the
natural parents as real and significant people in their adopted
child's prior-life experience.

Adoption Preparation Process

Adoptive applicants meet initially with an intake social
worker to address such issues as age, health, residency, religion, and fee. They are prepared for the group process, which
includes four or five couples and two social workers who meet
approximately 2 1/2 hours for eight sessions. Prior to the first
group meeting, the couples are given an outline of the sched-

ules and agendas for all meetings and the names of other group members. Each group member selects from the agenda one topic and assumes responsibility for introducing it to the group. Written autobiographies are shared with the group. Couples are involved in a role-playing exercise in which they assume the roles of adoptees, adoptive parents, and natural parents who release their children. Emphasis is placed on helping adoptive parents understand their responsibility in meeting the adoptees' needs for appreciation of their natural heritage and adoptive status.

Articles related to crucial issues for group discussion are assigned to group members. The final, formal assessment of each couple is not made until the group process is completed. The applicants must furnish marriage and birth certificates, medical reports, financial statements, and letters of reference as further evidence of their readiness for adoption. With positive completion of these materials, the couple and social worker will then meet to discuss the type of child they desire.

Birthparent Counseling Process

Birthparents are responsible for naming the child, completing the official birth record, and arranging for the transfer of the child to either a foster or adoptive home. Either before or after the child's birth, birthparents participate in selecting adoptive parents. Once the family has been selected, the birthparents prepare autobiographical and medical information about themselves and their families for the adoptive parents. They determine what kind of information they wish to provide for their child.

Birthparents must appear in court to give voluntary consent to the termination of parental rights before the child can be legally free for adoption. Social workers are responsible for giving birthparents information about this process.

Of the natural parents who make use of CSS counseling services relative to planning for their child, only a small percentage choose to release for adoption. CSS views adoption as an option. Release of a child for adoptive placement is viewed as being a responsible alternative, not a "selfless sacrifice."

Attitudes toward Openness

Catholic Social Services supports the definition of open adoptions given by the 1981 Ad Hoc Committee to Reevaluate Adoptive Placement Philosophy (see Chapter 2).

CSS views adoption as a unique institution within which both birthparents and adoptive parents have shared concerns and responsibilities. The agency emphasizes the importance of open communication between both sets of parents throughout the child's development. Adoption assures a child of a permanent, substitute family within which to grow and develop as a person. For adoptive parents, adoption is a way of becoming substitute parents to a child in need of a permanent family. For birthparents, adoption is a means by which they can be relieved of parenting responsibilities, with the understanding that in releasing the child, a constructive plan is being made for his or her future.

CHILD SAVING INSTITUTE

History

The Child Saving Institute of Omaha, Nebraska, has been offering varying degrees of openness in their adoptions for the past 18 years. Initially, openness consisted only of the exchange of non-identifying information, but at a later date evolved into the exchange of information and also pictures. Gradually the agency began facilitating gift giving by the birthparent to the adopted child. The movement, spurred on by the requests of birthparents, developed slowly, as the agency became increasingly satisfied with the responses of adoptive and birthparents to greater degrees of disclosure. At present, Child Saving Institute is primarily involved in the sharing of pictures and information and semiopen meetings. On occasion, they have also been involved in fully open adoptions.

Adoption Preparation Process

The first contact between the Child Saving Institute and the adoptive parents is usually a telephone conversation. If adoptive parents are interested in working with the agency, they are asked to send a letter expressing their specific interests about a child's age, sex, and other options they would be willing to consider. After submitting this letter, couples are invited to participate in orientation meetings. The initial preparation for prospective adoptive parents involves meetings with former adoptive and birthparents who have experienced varying degrees of openness. An integral aspect of the orientation is a panel presentation that includes birthparents, adoptees, and adult adoptees who tell their personal stories related to adoption. The workshop creates a sense of the vast number of options available to the adoptive parents and motivates them to carefully examine their attitudes, beliefs, and expectations.

Their views are discussed fully during the home-study process. During home studies, the family decides with a caseworker what kind of openness is most preferable to them. When couples are undecided, the agency gives them the names of families who have experienced differing kinds of adoption, so the prospective parents can hear their views about the advantages and disadvantages of different options. It is very important for the couple to develop a strong, trusting relationship with their worker during the home visits. This relationship is often crucial to the success of the first adoptive placement.

Couples are also asked to prepare albums that describe their families and lifestyles. Birthmothers may look at these albums when considering potential placements for their children. The degree of openness of the birthparents and the adoptive family is made on an individual basis depending upon the maturity, motivation, and psychological stability of the birthparents.

Birthparent Counseling Process

Counseling procedures reflect the philosophy that the role of the social worker is to clearly point out all alternatives so that birthparents have a sound basis on which to make decisions for their future and that of the unborn child. Counseling may center on personal problems, assistance with schooling, medical, legal, living arrangements, problems surrounding the pregnancy and whether to keep or to relinquish the child for adoption, and parenting issues. Adoption counseling involves a plan for the type of adoptive family the birthmother wants for her child. Characteristics given attention may include religion, race, and age. After the birthparents have decided on the nature of the adoptive placement they want for their child, the workers go through the list of approved candidates and choose two or three families who meet the description provided by the birthparents. Though birthparents may look at adoptive-family albums, the final decision about where the child will be placed is made by the agency.

In most cases, the placements have been made according to the mutual wishes of the birthparents and adoptive parents. Part of the adoption and birthparent preparation process is to provide extensive education about adoptive parents and the varying degrees of openness in adoption, and to assure the cooperation of the parties involved in achieving a mutually satisfying adoption experience.

Attitudes toward Openness

According to the Child Saving Institute, advantages of open adoption include alleviating the secrecy surrounding confidential adoptions and permitting children to have knowledge of their heritage and background. This is especially important in the area of medical information, so that adoptees will have knowledge of genetic factors that may influence their health. Disadvantages of open adoption are most often linked to social discomfort (with fully disclosed arrangements) and to the threats perceived in birthparents' having access to information about where their children are living and how they are doing. Though birthparents emphasize that their decision to place is evidence of their relinquishment of parental rights, society often views open arrangements as having the potential to create later difficulties and pain. The Child Saving Institute is careful to address this fear and asserts that openness is not synonymous with shared parenting, but is a means of facilitating greater support and trust among birthparents, adoptive parents, and adoptees.

CATHOLIC SOCIAL SERVICES FOR MONTANA

History

Catholic Social Services (CSS) for Montana has been offering fully disclosed adoptions for the past five years, and semiopen adoptions for the past ten years. For most of its history, CSS was strongly philosophically rooted in the practice of confidential adoptions, with policies similar to most adoption services affiliated with the Catholic church. The agency's transition toward the provision of more open forms of adoption has been a slow, evolutionary process.

Openness became featured as an option because of the agency's concerns for the adopted child and the birthparents. CSS recognized that many adoption practices were predicated upon the needs of birthparents and adoptive parents, with little regard for the later needs of the adopted child. The sharing of information, which characterizes semiopen and fully disclosed adoptions, was seen as a way of alleviating the mystery and secrecy that adoptees may sense about their backgrounds. CSS also realized that openness could help resolve issues that may later affect birthparents. An adoption worker at CSS described an incident involving a birthmother who waited 18 years to search for the son she had placed for adoption. She told the worker that she had prayed for the son each day since his placement. She later found out through the agency that he had died of pneumonia at age four. CSS views openness as a means of precluding such tragic experiences for birthparents.

The goal of openness is to provide an environment of trust

and honesty for all parties involved in the adoption, with the agency's confidence in their abilities to handle difficult situations. During 1986, 90 percent of the adoptions processed through CSS were open. Couples seeking to adopt children through CSS are advised that openness will be encouraged. Couples more interested in confidential adoptions usually register with another agency.

Adoption Preparation Process

The adoption preparation process for prospective adoptive parents includes completing applications and a personal biography, obtaining recommendations, attending a two-day workshop, and participating in home visits. Couples are asked to complete a variety of forms. They must submit marriage licenses, physical examination records from their doctors, and letters of recommendation from their priest or minister and members of the community. They are also asked to write an extensive autobiography, describing their backgrounds, relationships, goals, weaknesses, and views on parenting. Proof of infertility is also required.

When applications are submitted, couples are scheduled to attend a two-day workshop that addresses most issues involved in open adoptions. Topics covered include legal aspects of adoptions, infertility, parenting, and early bonding. Birthparents and adoptive parents who have chosen open adoptions discuss their experiences, and the prospective adoptive parents complete exercises that help them explore their feelings. The couples are encouraged to ask questions and discuss their apprehensions about the process. During the workshop Catholic Social Service workers tell the couples about the agency's expectations of their attitude and participation in the events and activities related to the openness practice. Workshops are held three or four times each year, and eight to ten couples attend each one. Most couples who have participated in the workshop have indicated that the workshop had a profound effect upon their decision to adopt.

When couples complete the workshop, they are asked to participate in a series of home studies. During home studies, adoptive parents are interviewed individually and as a couple. If it appears that the couple has a major difficulty with communication or some other problem, CSS works with them to resolve the conflict, rather than rejecting their application to be adoptive parents. Very rarely is a couple turned down without the agency intervening to correct the problems perceived. During the home visit couples are also asked whether they would be willing to provide shelter to a pregnant young woman until her baby is born. Because of possible pressures and ethical conflicts, there is a strict and absolute understanding that the couple will not be allowed to adopt the child whose mother has stayed in their home. After home visits and possible subsequent counseling are completed, the couple is eligible to adopt a child.

The openness practice offered by CSS is different from that of many other agencies. In order to remove any external pressure a birthmother may feel to place her baby, adoptive parents do not have any contact with her until the baby is born and she has made a final decision to place. The advantages of this approach include greater consideration of the right of the birthmother to make an independent choice and to avoid any disappointments adoptive parents may face if a birthmother changes her mind late in the adoption preparation process. Because of these guidelines, adoptive parents are never involved in the delivery or hospital stay.

Birthmother Counseling Process

Counseling for birthmothers who decide to place their babies through Catholic Social Services includes attention to the psychological and social aspects of pregnancy and adoption. The agency has four social workers who provide birthmother counseling.

Catholic Social Services prefers to begin intervention with birthmothers early in their pregnancies. Initial counseling focuses on the mother's attitude toward her pregnancy and how it will affect her current lifestyle and future. The birthmother who is interested in openness is given these options: she may tell the agency the kind of couple she wants to adopt her baby, choose the adoptive couple from profiles, and, after the baby is born, may meet the couple on a first-name basis, once. She has the opportunity to send letters and gifts to the adoptive family through the agency for as long as she desires. Further degrees of openness are dependent on agreements worked out between the birthmother and the adoptive parents. Birthmothers are seen for counseling every two weeks during the early stages of their pregnancy and every week as they approach delivery. Counselors emphasize the need for birthmothers to be aware of their responsibility for the decision to place and the later possible consequences of adoption. Counselors begin to work through the grieving process and pain that frequently coincide with the placement of a baby.

Birthmother counseling may also include intervention with the extended family of the birthmother and with the birthfather and his family wherever possible. Efforts are made to reach all parties closely involved with the birthmother and the placement. There are no "typical" family counseling situations, so workers are trained to be flexible and are prepared to deal with a vast array of complicated issues. These counseling sessions are especially significant in cases where the birthmother has emotional difficulties or has been the victim of child abuse or incest. One of the main goals of birthmother counseling is to encourage family members to be good to each other and respond in loving ways, regardless of the difficulty of their circumstances. Birthmothers receive counseling after the delivery and retain the option to keep their babies until they are home from the hospital.

Catholic Social Services also attempts to meet the material needs of the birthmother, which may include shelter, clothing, nutrition, and the payment of medical expenses. Birthmothers are given a large packet of materials containing information on pregnancy, health, nutrition, and the dangers of smoking or using drugs, and using alcohol during pregnancy. Shelter homes are available to birthmothers who are unable to live with their families or partners and have nowhere else to go. Several Catholic women's organizations make baby clothes and blankets and accept donations of maternity clothes and other items that may be needed by birthmothers. Catholic Social have assumed their roles in the adoption triad. As a result, the following options were added to the adoption process. The birthparent can (not required):

1. and is encouraged to spend time with the baby
2. name the child on the original birth certificate
3. learn the first name of the child and the first names of the adoptive parents
4. participate in the selection of the adoptive parents
5. have ongoing correspondence with adoptive parents (through the agency—no last names or addresses shared)
6. share a picture of her- or himself and extended family with adoptive parents
7. send a gift for the child

The adoptive parents can (not required):

1. learn first name(s) of birthparent(s)
2. partake in ongoing correspondence
3. send pictures of their child to the birthparent(s)
4. obtain pictures of birthparent(s) and extended family
5. obtain a more complete social and medical history on birth families

Beginning in the summer of 1981, both the San Antonio and Corpus Christi offices of LSST began a pilot project of offering an additional form of openness to prospective parents and birthparents—face-to-face meetings. Initially, these meetings were either taped or monitored by a social worker. However, as these meetings became more routine, monitoring ceased and adoptive parents and birthparents were allowed to share whatever they wished. Although the length of time spent together in these meetings is at the discretion of the parties involved, generally they last between one and two hours. As these meetings usually occur after placement, the adoptive parents often bring the child. After the meeting, social work-

Services may also advocate for birthmothers in the scho
tem so they will be better able to meet educational re
ments during their pregnancies.

For birthmothers who work with the agency, but de
keep their babies, similar efforts are made to facilitate a
awareness of the responsibility of parenting and to ma
propriate referrals to community resources.

Attitudes toward Openness

Catholic Social Services believes that openness in a
is the most humane, sensitive alternative available t
tive parents and birthparents willing to share infor
Openness requires a great deal of trust and acceptanc
can initially be threatening, but usually results in ve
fying relationships for all participants in the adopti
By offering openness, workers in adoption agencies re
much of the control they have traditionally maintai
cerning access to records and contact with birthpar
adoptive parents, allowing their clients to make deci
plans most appropriate to their individual needs.

LUTHERAN SOCIAL SERVICE OF TEXA
SAN ANTONIO

History

Open adoptions began in San Antonio through the
of letters between both sets of parents. Traditio
birthmother wrote a letter to the adoptive parents
educating adoptive couples on openness issues ar
them to consider some communication with the b
began in 1977. The procedure began with the excha
letter and later, ongoing correspondence. Once th
parents realized their children would have ques
started asking Lutheran Social Service of Texas
more information, including pictures. New optic
available as birthparents, adoptive parents, and
dividuals expressed their needs, frustrations, and h

ers meet separately with the adoptive parents and birthparents.

Adoption Preparation Process

Applications from prospective adoptive parents are taken in March and September each year. Secretaries screen for initial eligibility—applicants must have been married at least two years (three years if second marriage); be less than 45 years of age; have no more than one child living in the home; and provide evidence of infertility. Applicants meeting these requirements may be invited to a preadoption counseling session. This is a one-hour interview that primarily focuses on some of the myths of adoption, secrecy, attitudes about communication with birthparents, and most importantly, infertility issues. The key issue for readiness to adopt is whether the couple is dealing with their infertility.

Couples who are selected to begin the adoption preparation process attend a three-part seminar on adoption triad issues. The first session focuses on birthparents. Participants are required to read *The Adoption Triangle* (Sorosky, Baran, & Pannor, 1978). The second session focuses on adoptive-parent issues, such as infertility. The couples are required to read *The Wedded Unmother* (Halverson & Hess, 1980). A panel discussion is held with adoptive parents who have experienced an open adoption. The last session focuses on the adult adoptee. The assigned reading for this session is *Dear Birthmother* (Silber & Speedlin, 1982).

Throughout the seminar, options in openness are discussed, including: sharing first names; exchanging initial letters; exchanging pictures; birthmother selecting family; face-to-face meeting; ongoing correspondence. Most prospective parents want some form of openness after the seminar. Eighty to ninety percent of these families decide to meet the birthmother. Ninety percent of those who have met want only continuing correspondence.

Statewide, 200 families have met the birthparents since the option has been offered. About 80 families in San Antonio have had face-to-face meetings.

After the seminar, adoptive parents participate in follow-up interviews that involve individual and joint at-home visits. The adoptive applicants are also asked to prepare a social history, which birthparents use to select families.

Although the longest waiting time now is two years, some couples get a baby within weeks or months after approval. Twice as many couples apply as are actually chosen.

Birthparent Counseling Process

LSST secretaries are trained to take calls from birthmothers inquiring about the agency's program. LSST provides dormitory facilities and private-home care for birthmothers. The youngest birthmother in the San Antonio office was 11 and the oldest 49.

During the last month of the pregnancy, birthmothers have a chance to select an adoptive family. The staff selects five to six families from which the birthmothers may choose after reading their social histories. Reading social histories forces them to acknowledge the other set of parents and gives the birthmother a real role in selecting the adoptive parents. After placement, a copy of the social history of the adoptive family is given to the birthmother.

Birthmothers are offered all the options for openness. Most prefer to see the baby, and some opt to feed the infant. Placement may occur within 48–72 hours after birth. Birthmothers receive hospital counseling before and after delivery. Adoptive parents are notified only after the birthparent has signed the papers.

Face-to-face meetings may occur on placement day or later. Social workers for the adoptive parents and birthparents initially introduce the parties and then leave them for about one hour. The birthmother then brings the baby in to the adoptive parents.

Attitudes toward Openness

—The key to openness is realistic coping with adoption.

—The staff believes that many birthmothers would not place their babies unless there were at least some elements of openness. Many want an adoptive family who is willing to meet with them, even though they are uncomfortable with it at the time.

—Birthparents are given a real role in selecting the adoptive parents. This also forces the adoptive parents to acknowledge another set of parents.

—Face-to-face meetings serve to reaffirm the birthparents' decision in choosing a particular family.

—Adoption is painful for birthparents. Birthparents are helped to heal when they meet the loving, caring parents. Also, adoptive parents can explain to their adopted child that the birthmother is not rejecting, but is only concerned about him or her.

—The only negative that has been consistently reported has been other people's reactions to the meetings. Adoptive parents must continually educate others who labor under the myths about adoption.

—Birthparents are very protective of the family unit and would do nothing to disrupt it. They have a commitment to the family unit they have created.

—The agency assumes that the children will have better mental health because adoptive parents are coping with adoption realistically by providing their children with as much information as possible about their birthparents.

LUTHERAN SOCIAL SERVICE OF TEXAS: CORPUS CHRISTI

Adoption Preparation Process

Prospective adoptive parents are screened into the system based upon the preadoption counseling session with qualified applicants. They are educated about adoption and myths are dispelled. The worker then decides who will be invited to preadoption seminars. These seminars consist of 12 hours of group work.

Issues that must be dealt with in the seminar include:

—infertility grief work
—"total parent" issue (ownership of the child); adoptive parents must accept the fact that the child has two sets of parents

—threat and fear
—security
—sense of loss
—feeling empathy and understanding for the birthparents
—feeling empathy and understanding for the adoptees
—lack of control over lives
—ability to face feelings and deal with them
—trust

During the first day of the seminar, participants discuss feelings and experiences associated with infertility. Infertility is viewed as a loss of control over one's life, loss of the potential of a child that would be born, and a loss of health. The Kübler-Ross stages of grief work are discussed, and participants are made aware that they are not the only ones who are infertile. Applicants are then taken on a guided fantasy to help them gain empathy toward birthparents. They "walk through" a pregnancy and explain how they feel at each stage. They imagine what it is like to place a child for adoption and return home "with no baby." The group then is led in a discussion of the kinds of options for openness that birthparents might desire. The purpose of this exercise is to sensitize adoptive parents to the feelings of birthparents. Prospective parents are told that open adoptions were started out of concern for the children because it keeps them from thinking that they were rejected. Parents are told that asking birthparents to sign a paper and never know anything about the child is cruel and unusual punishment. To live with that anguish is not necessary.

A panel of birthmothers then discusses their various decisions and experiences regarding the open adoptions. Prospective parents are encouraged to ask the panel questions. According to Janet Cravens-Garner, the LSST Corpus Christi Regional Director, the group leader then explains that

> open adoption is like a marriage—you take it day by day. The relationship is built on trust, honor, integrity, commitment. If you have these qualities and have the best interests of the child

at heart—then it's ok. Ongoing relationship does not mean constant visits. Babysitting is unusual—but it happens. Birthparents need and want to know that the child is all right.

Group participants are then given a list of books to read prior to the next seminar including *The Wedded Unmother* (Halverson & Hess, 1980), *The Adoption Triangle* (Sorosky, Baran, & Pannor, 1978), and *Dear Birthmother* (Silber & Speedlin, 1982). The concluding part of the preadoption seminar lasts four hours. Discussion primarily focuses on telling the child about adoption; this includes role playing and talking with the child, using different approaches for different developmental levels. This exercise helps parents understand the positive value of open adoptions. They can tell their child "I met with the lady—there's a letter from her." "Adoptive parents, through the seminar, are forced to face what they are feeling. They sometimes think that they can just waltz in and walk out with a baby. This process is essential in helping them to get in touch with their real feelings," according to Cravens-Garner.

Birthparent Counseling Process

Clients come in generally around five to six months pregnant, usually considering adoption. Most are between 18 and 25 years of age. Of the approximately 120 birthmothers seen each year, about 25 to 30 percent choose adoption. The majority receive counseling services, but do not place.

Birthparent issues that must be dealt with include:

—Guilt over not parenting (not taking responsibility)

—Stages of grief

—Giving permission to feel and support as they experience their feelings

—Responsibility for the decision to relinquish; encourage the birthmother not to blame someone else

—Letting go; recognizing that the adoptive parent is the nurturing parent

—Secrecy

—Self-esteem (recognizing positives: positive choice of placing baby, giving birth to a beautiful baby, etc.)

—Grief work (requires time; requires talking about feelings). Birthparents have reached acceptance of their decision when they don't get teary every time they see a baby; when they feel that the child is someone else's baby; when they begin to pull back from the child and the adoptive family.

The first sessions are designed to give information about adoption and to break down myths. Open adoption is discussed from the beginning. Clients tend to be nervous that the agency will be judgmental and will try to trick them into placing the baby. If the woman places the baby, her expenses are paid. If she decides to parent the baby, she must pay the expenses.

Clients must discuss who to tell, how to tell, medical care, maternity clothes, education, birthfather, and their support system. They work on anticipating grief and discuss how to survive the loss of a loved one. Workers help the birthmother to break down the denial and face what is happening. They spend a session on each stage of grief work and read *How to Survive the Loss of a Love* (Colgrove, Bloomfield, & McWilliams, 1976). Often they also read *Dear Birthmother* (Silber & Speedlin, 1982) and handouts. They talk about past losses.

When close to delivery, the birthmother is asked to make both first and second choices of adoptive families for the baby. They also talk with other women who have placed and, through guided fantasy, talk about the future.

About 30 to 40 percent of the birthmothers choose not to have a face-to-face meeting. Approximately 95 percent choose the family, 95 percent see the baby, and 100 percent have a picture of the baby. Most clients participate in some degree of openness.

Attitudes toward Openness

—Refusal to participate in openness is viewed as denial.

—Concern was expressed over the birthparent getting short-changed in traditional adoptions. Adoptees are also not getting information about birthparents.

—The birthmother usually dictates if the face-to-face meeting will occur at placement. The agency is very flexible. Most face-to-face meetings happen two weeks to one month after placement.

—Workers have never seen any negative outcomes of open adoptions. However there have been situations when the adoptive parent may want one kind of situation and the birthparent may want another.

—Ongoing visitation is *not* the most common arrangement.

—Open adoptions are much more work than traditional adoptions. It is necessary to do more social work and to help the family work through their feelings.

—Social workers lose more control in open adoptions.

LUTHERAN SOCIAL SERVICE OF TEXAS: AUSTIN

History

Nine to twelve years ago there were no options for birthparents to meet adoptive parents. Birthmothers routinely entered the hospital under an assumed name and adoptions were cloaked in secrecy. Gradually, the LSST Austin office began to show adoptive parent profiles to their birthmothers, then began to offer other clients options, including exchanging letters and pictures. Face-to-face meeting options became available in April, 1983.

There are no set rules regarding openness, and options are tailored to individual family needs. Birthmothers have a wide range of options, including seeing the baby in the hospital, rooming in, nursing the baby, sending gifts with the child, and choosing the family.

Most birthmothers are involved in reviewing profiles of adoptive families and selecting the adoptive family. Out of 35 adoptions in 1987, 55 to 60 percent of the birthmothers were involved in the selection of the adoptive parents. There were 12 face-to-face meetings; all were held within three months to one year after placement. None occurred at the time of placement, and last names and locations were not exchanged in these meetings.

Adoption Preparation Process

To qualify for adoption, applicants must be under 45 years of age, have no more than one child living at home, and be unable to have children or advised by a doctor not to have children. Of the 150 applications LSST Austin receives each year, about 30–40 are accepted. Lutherans are given first consideration in most cases.

Applicants attend a one-day seminar in which issues unique to adoption are discussed. Participants discuss their fears about adoption, the impact a child will have on their lives, life-span issues for the adoptive family, explaining adoption to a child at different levels of cognitive development, and concerns about searching. A videotape is presented that depicts birthmothers talking about contacts with adoptive parents. Parents are told that most LSST clients have ongoing communication, but not ongoing contacts.

After the seminar, prospective parents are interviewed individually and jointly. A home visit is scheduled next. During these meetings, couples are asked if they could be open to sharing pictures or meeting the birthparents. Being willing to have an open adoption does not affect approval or waiting time. Seventy percent of the adoptive couples are interested in open adoptions and are willing to meet if the birthmother wants it.

Attitudes toward Openness

—LSST staff do not recommend that children have ongoing contact, but do not see anything destructive in it.

—Most of the time birthparents choose not to have ongoing contact because of their concern for the child having divided loyalties.

—Updated material is made available, as most clients have ongoing communication.

—Often birthparents lose the fantasy that the child is "my baby" once they see the baby a year or so later and realize that the baby belongs to another family and is no longer theirs.

SUMMARY

Agencies provide intensive preparation for adoptive parenthood, but the messages given about openness vary among agencies and even among regional offices within the same agency. There appears to be a lack of understanding and communication among and within agencies about the practice of open adoptions. The term provokes a great deal of emotion, and agencies either tend to be totally for or against the practice.

In reality, however, even agencies who claim to be against open adoptions indicate that they practice some degree of openness in adoptions. In some agencies, for example, the practice of birthparents meeting noncorresponding adoptive parents is viewed as a form of openness, whereas other agencies view the sharing of nonidentifying information and pictures as an aspect of open adoptions. Others view face-to-face meetings and ongoing contact between corresponding birth and adoptive families as open adoptions.

Some agencies view adoption as a lifelong process that involves the adoptee, birthparents, and adoptive parents, while others see adoption as principally involving only the adoptive parents and adoptees. Traditional adoption agencies tend to see the role of a birthparent as ending and the role of adoptive parent as beginning at placement. On the other hand, advocates of open adoption see adoption as an institution that may involve the adoptee and two sets of parents.

Desperate families desiring to have children tend to espouse whatever position their agency has taken on adoption in order to receive a child. The type of adoptive parent education and counseling provided seems to directly influence adoptive parents toward or away from openness. Even in agencies that purport to offer a choice, adoptive parents are likely to favor openness if they feel it will hasten the process of getting a baby. Moreover, if couples prefer a style of adoption that does not fit with the agency's perspective, generally they are discouraged from continuing to work with that agency.

Agencies also vary in the type of preparation given for adoptive parenthood. Agencies specializing in confidential adoption use casework and introductory group meetings, while some agencies advocating open adoption tend to use group work as the primary means for adoption preparation. Agencies using group work tend to be more process oriented, client centered, and tend to involve the participants more in their own learning. Most of these agencies tend to give the birthparents copies of the adoptive parents' self-description or social history to assist them in selecting a family for their child. However, one agency notes that this may be counterproductive because the process puts a great deal of pressure on the adoptive parents to sell themselves.

Grief regarding infertility and relinquishing a child seem to be important issues that are addressed in all agencies studied. However, agencies offering primarily confidential adoptions tend to believe that open adoptions prolong the grieving process by not bringing closure to the birthparent's experience of relinquishing. Advocates of open adoption believe that openness helps birthparents reach a quicker acceptance of their loss.

Advocates of open adoptions also stress empathic understanding of birthparents and that adoptive parenting is different from birthparenting. They tend to have a more positive view of birthparents than advocates of confidential adoption. Many view birthparents as making a moralistic choice designed to benefit the child. As a result, the birthparents have a commitment to the family unit and would not be disruptive. Proponents of confidential adoptions tend to assume that birthparents are unpredictable and may, if given the chance, try to reclaim the child.

Issues of trust and responsibility seem paramount in open adoptions. For example, Catholic Social Services of Green Bay emphasizes adoptive parent responsibility for meeting adoptees' needs through an appreciation of his or her natural heritage and adoptive status. Responsibility is given to birthparents and adoptive parents to decide whether identifying information will be shared. Birthparents are given the responsibility for selecting adoptive parents. Some compare open adoptions to a marital relationship as both are based on honor, integrity, and commitment. However, confidential adoption practice is based on the assumption that professional social workers should be in charge and be responsible for decision making.

As open adoptions practice is relatively recent, the future outcomes of such placements, with respect to the child, are difficult to predict. However, the open adoptions agencies surveyed report no negative experiences so far. All of the agencies tend to stress the advantages of openness for birthparents and adoptees and place relatively less emphasis on the advantages of openness for the adoptive parents.

Some agencies acknowledge that the practice was instituted to increase agency placements, as they believe that many birthparents would not relinquish through an agency if open placements were not offered. Moreover, due to the great demand for children, adoptive parents are generally viewed as not being in a bargaining position. Confidential adoption agencies tend to believe that many of their adoptive parents and birthparents would not seek agency services if confidential adoption were not available. However, regardless of the rationale for the various agency practices regarding open adoptions, all of the agencies concur that there is a need for research on this topic.

5
Method

PARTICIPANTS

The participants in the study included 17 adoptive couples who had adopted one or more infants through the Austin, San Antonio, or Corpus Christi offices of Lutheran Social Service of Texas, Inc. (LSST). Six families came from Austin, five from San Antonio, and six from Corpus Christi. Interviews were also conducted with 15 birthparents, and one birthgrandmother, and one birthfather corresponding to the adoptive families. The adoptive parents had 11 male and 13 female adopted children ranging in age from four months to six years at the time of the study.

The sample included 15 Caucasian and two Hispanic adoptive couples. The adoptive mothers ranged in age from 31 to 42 years, and the adoptive fathers from 30 to 47 years. Birthparent ages (at the time of the birth of their child) ranged from 14 to 42 years of age. All adoptive families were middle to upper-middle class, based on family income.

PROCEDURE

From a listing of adoptive parents and birthparents provided by three LSST regional offices, five adoptive families
and five alternate adoptive families (with corresponding
birthparents) from each of the three sites were randomly selected for study participation by the researchers. Staff from
the LSST offices then contacted and identified the adoptive
parents and birthparents willing to participate in the study.
At the time of the interview, each participant signed a written
consent form.

Almost all adoptive parents were interviewed at the LSST
office through which they had adopted. Each couple was interviewed jointly. Birthparents were individually interviewed in
one of the LSST offices. In two cases, the adoptive parents
were interviewed in their homes. All of the interviews were
audiotaped and transcribed. Because three birthparents lived
out of state, they were interviewed by telephone. One birthparent, due to illness, also has to be interviewed by telephone.

INSTRUMENTATION AND DATA ANALYSIS

Data were collected and qualitatively analyzed by using a
separate, semistructured interview for the adoptive parents
and birthparents. On the basis of the type of adoption chosen,
the families were divided into three groups. There were two
confidential (closed) adoptive families, five semiopen (shared
information or one-time meeting) adoptive families and ten
fully disclosed (ongoing contact) adoptive families.

The following issues were examined in the data analysis:

A. Type of adoption chosen
B. Reasons for choosing option
C. Perceived advantages and disadvantages of confidential, semi-
   open, and fully disclosed adoption
D. Satisfactions encountered in the type of adoption chosen
E. Perceived impact of type of adoption chosen on all parties (child,
   adoptive parents, and birthparents)

F. Rights of parties involved in adoption

G. Advice for prospective adoptive parents or for someone considering placing a child for adoption

Complete lists of the interview questions for both the adoptive parents and birthparents are contained in the appendixes.

6

Results: Family Profiles

Profiles of the 17 families who participated in the study were developed from the analyses of the transcripts of their interviews. These interviews were examined in order to determine the level of openness in the adoption and the birthparents' and adoptive parents' attitudes surrounding the degree of openness they had selected.

The families were divided into three groups, based on the degree of openness in their adoption. The first group, families with confidential adoptions, had no openness in their situations. There was little or no information shared among the adoptive parents and birthparents, and no ongoing contact of any kind was present. When an attempt was made to contact the birthmothers for participation in this study, no response was received. The second group, families with semiopen adoptions, had exchanged such items as pictures, gifts, or letters with birthparents. In one case, a face-to-face meeting had taken place, but no identifying information was shared and no ongoing contact was maintained. The third group, families with fully disclosed adoptions, had ongoing contact between adoptive parents, birthparents, and the children.

This chapter presents and illustrates issues associated with each of these types of adoptions. Families sharing certain attitudes or qualities regarding openness were clustered, and case vignettes were developed and identified with pseudonyms. A few actual quotes are included, but concrete characterizations have been obscured in order to protect the confidentiality of individual families who participated in the study. The vignettes of four families presented in this chapter illustrate major themes and describe family dynamics in the confidential, semiopen, and fully disclosed adoption situations studied.

FAMILIES WITH CONFIDENTIAL ADOPTIONS

Two families had very confidential, closed adoptions. One family had two adopted children, aged three and six. The other family had one adopted child, aged three. Neither family was offered a choice about the degree of openness in the adoption. Neither birthmother was interviewed because no response to requests for their participation in the study was received.

Both families strongly favored confidential over open adoption. They indicated that they would feel more secure not knowing the birthmother. Both feared that the birthmother might take the child back (and that the courts might cooperate in this) if she had any contact with the child. They indicated that openness would be confusing to the child, especially when he or she was young. They also felt that they did not want anyone "looking over your shoulder" once the adoption was finalized. The only disadvantage of confidential adoption, they felt, was that the child might find it harder to locate a birthparent if he or she should search.

When asked about potential advantages of open adoption, both families felt that there were few. The only advantages were seen to be for the child, and only when the child was older. No advantages were seen for either the adoptive parents or the birthparents. Little empathy for the birthmother was shown in either case, and neither adoptive couple saw themselves as benefiting from knowing the birthmother.

Fear of the birthmother and lack of willingness to address

adoption as an ongoing family issue are illustrated in the following quotes:

— "We don't really think about the adopted part of it very often."

— "I feel like they're my kids without any ifs, ands, or buts about it."

— "I don't think about the fact that they're adopted that often."

— "I consider them my children and this is my way of raising them and I'm not answerable to anybody, whereas I feel like if it was an open adoption, I might be paranoid enough to think that they're judging me."

— "Some liberal people think that they can handle all this [openness] but I personally wouldn't want to."

— "We have to go through all this [the rigamarole of adoption proceedings] to have one, and I think with open adoption, it would keep that wound open."

Some of these attitudes were also reflected in the couples' responses to questions about the rights of the parties involved. Both couples felt that birthparents had no legal rights. One couple felt that birthparents did have a right to inquire of the agency about the upbringing of their child. Both couples felt that the adoptive parents' rights were the same as those of biological parents: "the right to be a parent without interference from outside agencies or otherwise, other authority figures." Both couples felt that adopted children had a right to know as much as they want about their background and to find out who their birthparents are.

Adoptive parents' attitudes about their child's searching reflected concern and a feeling of being threatened. One couple felt that their children would search, but they anticipated a negative experience for their children and wanted to protect them from it. The other couple felt that their child was well adjusted and would therefore not be overly curious about birthparents: "It's not going to be a big deal to him." If he did wish to search, they wanted to do it as a family rather than for him to do it on his own.

FAMILIES WITH SEMIOPEN ADOPTIONS

Five families had semiopen adoptions. These included all cases in which biological and adoptive parents had only shared pictures or letters with nonidentifying information (four cases), or in which one face-to-face meeting had occurred with no sharing of identifying information (one case).

When asked about the advantages of confidential adoption, the adoptive parents' responses were suggestive of a fear of the birthmother and a negative, stereotypical view of her. For example, adoptive parents noted that it was more comfortable not to know the birthmother, that they felt protected from the emotional distress of knowing her, that it would be less confusing to the child, and that they would be able to develop a positive fantasy about the birthmother.

When asked about the disadvantages of confidential adoption, adoptive parents commented that they would not be able to meet the birthparents, and that the adopted child would be more likely to search if little were known about his or her birthparents. Birthmothers regretted that they would not get to know their child directly, and they would always be going through a third party. They noted that the child would always wonder who his or her birthparents were. Likewise, adoptive parents expressed empathy for the birthparents: "You walk out of the hospital with nothing; you never hear what happens to the child; you go crazy."

When asked about the advantages of open adoption, adoptive parents indicated the following: it would fulfill their curiosity about the child's birthparents, it would be easier to explain adoption to the child, it would make the birthparents real people, and it would ease the birthparents' fears about their child's well-being. Birthparents stated that the child would be able to understand where they came from and that they were really loved. Birthparents also felt that they would be able to see and know the child, although they would need to be strong, mature, and know what they were doing; and that they would get to fulfill their curiosity about the adoptive parents.

Disadvantages of open adoption also were cited by adoptive

parents. They noted that it would be scary to meet the birth-mother, that the birthmother might become a pest, that it could do harm to the child, and that the birthparents and adoptive parents might not like each other, which might cause the birthmother to reconsider her adoption plan and decide to keep the baby. In addition, they noted that, "if we met the birth-mother and didn't like something, we may look for that trait in the child and hold it against the child." Despite the disad-vantages of openness, however, the adoptive parents' over-riding concern was to adopt: "If open was the only way we could, then maybe." Although most birthmothers saw no dis-advantages to open adoption, some saw disadvantages if the birthmother was weak, or that it would be all right as long as identifying information was not shared: "Otherwise, she might want to steal the child back."

The perceived advantages and disadvantages just cited are consistent with the satisfactions and difficulties that the re-spondents noted with their semiopen adoptions. In terms of satisfactions, the adoptive parents were pleased to know that the birthmother had information about the well-being of the baby and that the birthmother had matured herself; however, "The less I know, the better." The birthmothers were pleased to have information about their children and to feel secure that the adoptive parents were happy as well.

The difficulties with semiopen adoptions cited by the adop-tive parents included fear that the birthmother might want the child back and problems that might occur when much more information is available on one child's birthmother than on a sibling's. The birthmothers were pleased to have information, but they seemed to want more: "You always want to have a little bit more"; "You don't get to know the child directly, you always have to go through a third party"; "Giving up the child, seeing the picture drives you crazy. You want to see more. It helps to see pictures, but it's hard too. My only joy is knowing I'll see her some day." One birthmother had taken photos of her daughter and had life-sized enlargements made for hang-ing in her room.

Adoptive parents and birthparents with semiopen arrange-ments differed in some important ways on their views of the rights of the members of the adoption triad. The adoptive parents felt that birthparents had no rights. At most, they had a right to information about the child. The birthparents felt that they had a right to information about their child, expressed a longing to meet the child when he or she was older, and even wished to become responsible for the child if something happened to the adoptive parents.

Adoptive parents felt that their own rights were the same as those of any parent, "complete: we can raise the child as our own." Birthparents felt that the adoptive parents had the right to information about the child's background and to their own privacy. However, no birthmothers mentioned the right of adoptive parents to raise the child completely as their own.

In terms of the rights of the adopted child, adoptive parents felt that they were entitled to information about their background and to find their birthparents when they were older. Birthmothers noted the same right to information, but also stated that the child should be able to choose to live with them, if they wished.

As they discussed the anticipated impact that sharing would have on the members of the adoption triad, responses suggested a mixture of empathy and fear. For example, adoptive parents felt good that the birthmother would know that her child was healthy. However, this feeling was mixed with the fear that seeing a picture might make the birthmother want her child back: "I felt like a rat upon meeting the birthmother for the first time. It was so emotionally charged. I had this woman's child and she was leaving without the child. All those changes that your body goes through—you have those feelings, but not the baby."

In general, both adoptive parents and birthparents in semiopen arrangements were quite empathic with regard to each others' needs. The adoptive parents were pleased that the birthmothers had information, and the birthmothers were pleased to know of their child's status. However, this empathy was mixed with the adoptive parents' fear that the birthmothers might want to reclaim their children. The birthmothers actually did express a desire for more complete contact with their children, and in some cases, fantasies that the child would come to live with them.

The following vignette describes a family who has one semiopen and one confidential adoption. Issues surrounding the decision to have a face-to-face meeting with their second child's birthmother are presented.

Roger and Donna Anderson

Mr. and Mrs. Roger Anderson have two children, Cynthia, aged four, and Karen, aged two, who were adopted as infants. Roger Anderson is a 37-year-old computer programmer and Donna Anderson is a 39-year-old housewife. They both have college degrees.

(Mrs. Anderson speaking)

We had always wanted children and I was unable to have any. I guess we had been married about ten years when we finally decided to pursue adoption. We had friends who had adopted through Lutheran Social Service of Texas, so we decided to call the agency.

First, we were invited to a get-acquainted meeting and then to another meeting in which we were essentially told that the agency had decided to work with us. The worker told us what to expect in the adoption-study process and notified us that we would be attending a seminar a few weeks later. During the seminar, we heard all of these couples talking about how they had tried unsuccessfully for years to become pregnant but had been unable to. Roger and I, for the first time, really realized that we were like them and would probably never have our own children. This was very traumatic for us. We later saw a tape of birthmothers talking and learned what it means to them to relinquish a child for adoption.

We completed the seminar and a few weeks later the agency finished our study and approved us for adoption. We had no preference for the sex of the child—we just wanted a baby. About four weeks passed before we received a call indicating that we had one. We adopted Cynthia when she was three days old. I think her birthmother was a college student around 23. We were given her medical history and some information about her background. The birthmother wrote a letter to Cynthia and in it she said that she came from a loving family herself and she wanted Cynthia to have the same opportunities that she had. This was something she couldn't give her at the time. I don't know much more about her past—I do have a biographical sketch but I don't remember everything that is on it. I think Cynthia's father had dropped out of college and was working. I think Cynthia weighed about six pounds at birth. It's funny because if you give birth yourself naturally, you probably remember all these things down to her foot size. I can't. I have to go review the file.

When we adopted Cynthia, we were not given any real options for openness. I don't think the agency was offering open placements then very much. Anyway, I wasn't really for the idea. I had always believed in an adoption where anonymity is preserved. I didn't want to know who the biological mother was and didn't want her to know who we were.

During the placement process, as we were looking at Cynthia's medical records, I noticed that an attempt was made to blot out the birthmother's name with ink. However, I could make out some of the letters. I first looked at it out of curiosity and then became angry with myself as I realized I didn't want to know her name. I have now blocked all of the letters out of my mind. I don't remember the name at all.

With our second adoption, Karen, things were a little different. We attended a seminar and the subject of open adoption came up frequently. I had very negative feelings about it at first. Unlike our first seminar, this time we met with birthmothers who had relinquished their children for adoption and I got a different view of the trauma that biological mothers actually go through. I had always, I guess, in my mind, been threatened by the thought that the biological mother might change her mind and want to take the child back, and I wanted to do everything to avoid that. Also, there was a certain amount of resentment that I felt at that time—that biological mothers might come back 20 years after having not had any contact at all and not sharing any of the responsibilities or the trauma of raising kids and then want to horn in on it. But when I heard the birthmothers discuss their feelings, I realized that was pretty ridiculous.

At first, Roger didn't want to meet our children's birthparents either because he felt that if there was something in the mother that he didn't like, he would somehow hold that against the child or look for that trait in the child. He was afraid it would negatively affect his relationship with the child.

The agency told us all about open adoptions, but we still were not interested. They told us about our various options. We knew that some people have face-to-face contact with their birthmothers and some visit regularly. We were uncomfortable with this, but we did decide that it might be OK to meet once at placement, if the birthmother insisted, and write her through the agency. We were also told that we would be matched with a birthmother who also wanted this arrangement.

When we received the call about Karen's birth, we were told that the birthmother had requested to meet us and keep in touch with us through LSST. We figured that this arrangement would be least disruptive to our family and to our child.

Needless to say, we were very nervous on placement day. Before we saw Karen, our worker prepared us for a meeting with her birthmother. We were told that we would have about 30 to 45 minutes to talk with her and to get all our questions answered. Our feelings ranged from joy that she was giving us her baby to fear that she would find out too much about us. When she entered the room, we just stared. She wasn't at all like what we had feared. She was a scared vulnerable girl who was making the most difficult decision of her life.

Once we began to visit with her, we realized that she was just as apprehensive as we were. She only wanted to meet the people she had picked to raise her baby. We told her all about our family and about our other daughter, Cynthia. She seemed happy that Karen would have a big sister and asked that we send family pictures from time to time. We agreed to exchange letters monthly through the agency. I couldn't believe we were saying that—but it just seemed right at the time. I remembered that our worker had said that many families have ongoing correspondence and that this is a preferred way of handling adoptions.

Now, we both have a very positive feeling about both of the birthmothers. They both, I think, were basically very good people. You know, one was a college student and they both seemed to have been responsible people. I feel grateful toward them right now and I feel like I love them. I can pass that positive feeling on to Cynthia and Karen.

Over the past two years, we have exchanged about ten let-

ters. In the beginning we wrote monthly, but now I guess we
are all so busy that we just write every two or three
months. I imagine that, eventually, we will only keep in touch
at Christmas- and birthday-time. That sort of bothers us, though,
because we actually like Karen's birthmother and want to stay
fairly close.

We do fear, though, that Cynthia one day might not like it if
we are writing to Karen's birthmom and we don't have any
contact with hers. We'll have to tell her that the situations differed and that her birthmother did not wish any contact when
she was placed for adoption. Our worker told us, though, that
if Cynthia's mother ever did contact the agency seeking correspondence, we would be notified. As far as we are concerned,
that would be great.

Patricia Murphy: Karen Anderson's Birthmother

Patricia Murphy, Karen's birthmother, is a 21-year-old college graduate. She is planning to enter graduate school next
year. Her career goal is to become a psychologist.

(Patricia Murphy speaking)
I was 19 when Karen was born. I had been dating her father
since high school and always thought we would get married.
When I got pregnant, he really freaked out. He was finishing
college and had been admitted to law school. The last thing he
wanted was a child. I knew I didn't want to raise a baby alone
so I decided to place her for adoption. I saw an ad in the paper
about LSST and called the agency when I was about five months
pregnant. At the time I thought it (the adoption) would be easy
to handle; but the further along I was with my pregnancy, the
harder the decision was. I knew that if I did place her, I had
the option of ongoing contact and/or a face-to-face meeting. I
knew if I did give up the baby I would want to meet the family
at least once, so when I was given social histories on potential
families, I selected a couple who seemed very caring and were
agreeable to meeting me.

My worker kept telling me that the final decision was totally
up to me. She said that I didn't have to give up the baby, that
I should make a decision based upon what was best for both of

us. Ed, the baby's father, was really pushing me to place her. I didn't really make up my mind until I was in the hospital with her. Right after she was born, I remember holding her, stroking her blonde hair and looking at her sleeping peacefully in my arms. I knew then that I wanted everything to be right for her. It wasn't fair for me to keep her. She deserved better. When the worker came to visit me that day, I said that I had definitely decided to place her for adoption. When I told her, I immediately felt at peace. It was a good feeling, to have made a decision. I also felt sad, but I knew I was doing what was best for her.

While in the hospital, I named her Catherine Suzanne. I knew they would change her name, but I wanted to name her anyway—after all she was mine, if only for a short while. I told the worker that I would like to meet her adoptive parents on placement day. She said that I could talk with them briefly first, and then place the baby in their arms during the service. I cried.

I'll never forget the day I first saw her adoptive parents. They were just like I had pictured them. He was tall, slender, and very well dressed. She had a small build and was very attractive. As I was assessing them, I'm sure they were comparing me to their fantasy about what I would be like. We talked at length about my background, and they told me all about their family. I said that I wanted to keep in touch with them and would like to know how my baby was doing. They said they would write and send pictures to their worker who would forward them to me. I was pleased they seemed so giving and understood how difficult this placement was for me. When I asked them what they planned to name Catherine, they hesitated momentarily before responding, "Karen." I liked the name, but always knew she would be Catherine to me.

I told them all about my pregnancy and explained how difficult it had been for me to decide to place my baby. Tears came to their eyes as I talked with them about how very much I wanted the baby to know I loved her. They reached over and we all shared a big hug. They promised to always keep in touch and to share my feelings with her once she was old enough to understand. During the placement service, I held my baby for the last time. I kissed her good-bye and whispered to her new parents that I hoped one day that we could all meet again.

I would have liked more face-to-face meetings, but I don't

think I am emotionally ready to handle it now. It's so hard to give up a child, anyway. But, I know when I receive the letters and pictures of her—I go crazy. It is so hard to love someone that you know you can no longer have. But I prefer this arrangement to a confidential adoption when I would not even know if she was alive and well. At least I know what her parents look like. I'm glad we never exchanged names. If we did, I would be tempted to want her back. I bet her parents might fear that I would try to take her back, too. I really wouldn't, though—I know she is better off where she is and I am better off getting on with my life and knowing that she is happy.

Families choosing semiopen placements tend to empathize with the birthparents' need to have some kind of information on the status of their children. This understanding seems to develop through preplacement contact with birthmothers who have relinquished children. Through this interaction, myths and stereotypes of both birthparents' and adoptive parents' motives and attitudes are often dispelled.

Although apprehensive at first, both parties generally become comfortable with receiving direct communication and personal information about each other, while maintaining the anonymity traditional in adoptive placements. Adoptive parents and birthparents tend to agree that such ongoing contact is preferable for the children as they mature and become more inquisitive about their genetic background. In the preceding case illustration, the family acknowledges that the differential contact with the two birthparents may be problematic as the children mature and compare their adoptive background information.

In this type of adoption, the agency serves as mediator, advisor, and transmitter of information between the parties. The agency maintains contact with both parties, therefore, and a trained social worker is aware of the interactional dynamics, as well as any issues and concerns that arise over the years after placement.

FAMILIES WITH FULLY DISCLOSED ADOPTIONS

Ten families had fully disclosed adoptions, which are defined as including the sharing of identifying information among birthparent(s) and adoptive parents, with ongoing personal contact of some type.

When asked about the advantages of confidential adoption, most adoptive parents stated that there were none, except in cases where a birthparent was "crazy" or "not the kind you would want visiting you." The only advantages cited were for people who could not cope with the meeting and that you would not have people visiting so often. The advantages noted by birthparents were that confidential adoptions made it possible to pretend that the birth never happened, to be less close to the child and, consequently, to feel less pain, and to provide the protection that might be needed by some people.

From the adoptive parents' point of view, the disadvantages of confidential adoption were that it would be unfair to the child (lack of information, child may fantasize) or unfair to the birthparents (they would worry, think the worst had happened). No advantages to the adoptive parents were cited. Birthparents likewise cited disadvantages both to themselves and the children: something would be missing in the child's life, it would prey on insecurities, and the adoptive parents would have deprived their adopted children of something that is really special. Their views were quite strong: "I think it's the pits and I think it should be stopped immediately"; "It's something that is forbidden and shameful to the birthmother."

The following advantages of open adoptions were cited by the adoptive parents: it is in the best interest of the child to have information; their relationship with the birthmother was positive; if you know birthparents, "you don't have to fear they would snatch the children"; and you know what sort of people the birthparents are. One sentiment expressed was, "Do it for the children." One couple said, "We feel good about ourselves in showing the birthparent family that we are doing a good job of raising a child." Birthparents noted that openness means that they have no fear, no unknowns, and an honest relationship. When a birthmother has nightmares or dreams, she can pick up the phone and see how the child is. "You have a bond with the family through the child." "He'll always be able to relate back to where he's really from—his parents. If he has questions, he'll be able to ask me. It's the perfect solution." At the same time, some birthparents expressed an interest in overseeing the raising of their children.

Although many adoptive parents saw no disadvantages to openness, two primary concerns emerged: (1) the problem of the additional time and effort required to maintain the relationship and (2) the need to have a mature birthmother. Some sentiments expressed by adoptive parents, in regard to these concerns, were: "In the future, it will make demands on our time and cut into our social life. I'm not so sure I would do this open thing again"; "If [the birthmother] were a different person, she might be intrusive." The disadvantages in openness cited by birthparents centered around the continuing pain they experience in seeing their child: "You have a tendency to think, "Gee, if I had only kept her"; "Getting close and knowing you can't have him—he's not yours"; "If you want it back more and more, you just have to discipline yourself."

Most adoptive parents in the study chose fully disclosed openness with ongoing contact because they felt it was in the best interests of the child. Although they did not feel that they were offered the option of having a confidential adoption, they typically started out with a semiopen situation and gradually progressed to fully disclosed openness, as they established a relationship with the birthparent(s). Some adoptive parents were strongly in favor of their situation: "It's the right thing for *all* adoptive parents." Birthparents chose openness because they wanted to know how the child was and wanted the child to know them. One birthparent said, "I would have kept the child if I couldn't have openness—I can't imagine not knowing where the baby is and how she's doing." Another birthmother noted that she became attached to the baby in the hospital and couldn't let him go.

When adoptive parents discussed the perceived impact openness would have, they noted that the child would have information and less pain, and that the birthmother would know about the child and would have adults to talk to. However, when discussing the impact on their own situations, several reservations were expressed:

—"Sometimes I think I'm tired of sharing. It's getting ready for the visits. The kids will fight and punch each other and you say, 'Oh Lord, please don't do this in front of them.' When they leave, I say, 'Whew, that's another visit over with.'"

—"It's OK, as long as we can control it."

—"Once the paper is signed, birthparents have no rights except what we agreed to. Even if I were threatened, I'd have to stand by it."

When birthparents were asked about the perceived impact on the child, they noted that the child would know where he or she came from and would understand the birthparent's motives in placing the child. "It's the best thing I could do for the child," remarks one birthparent. For themselves, birthparents noted that they liked having an extended family. One noted that she planned to use the adoptive mother as a support unit when she had her own children. At the same time, they noted challenges in fearing that the child would not like them or in explaining to later children who this birthchild was. The perceived impact on adoptive parents was primarily in terms of information about the child.

Adoptive parents and birthparents differed to some degree on their perceptions of the rights of members of the adoption triad. Concerning the rights of birthparents, adoptive parents felt they had the right to know that the child was healthy and loved. However, they felt that they were in control of the birthparents' rights: "The adoptive parents decide the birthparents' rights"; "They [the birthparents] have no official rights—we should give back the rights once the child reaches maturity"; "She has a right to see the child as long as she doesn't impose herself on us." Although birthparents realize that they gave up their rights, one noted that she had the right to love and to discipline her child.

Adoptive parents felt that their children had the right to know as much as possible about their birthparents and to know their heritage. One adoptive father noted that the child's rights should supersede those of the birthparents, especially if they needed medical information. When rights conflict, however, they should be judged on a case-by-case basis by an intermediary. Birthparents felt that the children had the right to information and to know them. One birthmother said that the child had the right to come live with her.

Adoptive parents felt that their rights were the same as those of other parents. In addition, one father noted that the adoptive parents had the right not to have laws overturned retroactively so that the birthmother could reclaim her child. Birthparents felt that the adoptive parents had the right to be the child's parents and make decisions. However, one birthmother said, "If I legally could, I would take the adoptive mother to court. They have all the rights once the papers are signed."

In terms of satisfactions, adoptive parents felt that openness was good for the child, that there were no questions or secrecy, that they had peace of mind in knowing everything, and that they had a personal relationship with the birthmother. In several cases, the adoptive parents suggested that agreeing to openness was a sacrifice on their parts: "Out of our love, the child's questions are going to be answered"; "We have allowed her [the birthmother] to come into our family"; "Open adoption requires extra effort. You have to be willing to suffer." Birthparents cited the same satisfaction; being pleased to know that the child was taken care of and had information and having a relationship with the adoptive parents.

Difficulties were cited by both adoptive parents and birthparents. The adoptive parents felt uncomfortable seeing the affection and pain expressed by the birthparents. In one case, a mother noted concern that their arrangement was too open, "so that there will be problems with her wanting to come around later on." Another challenge was noted by families who only had an open situation with one of their children's birthmothers. Birthparents cited their ongoing grief at seeing the child: leaving the child was difficult, knowing that the adoptive parents are in control of the relationship was painful. "I feel like I'm her mom and I ought to be able to pick her up and take her with me any time I want to." Several birthparents hoped that, later on, their children would come to live with them.

In summary, both adoptive parents and birthparents who had chosen fully disclosed openness felt that the arrangement was potentially very positive for the child. The child would have background information about his or her past; he or she would have a relationship with the birthparent, which birthparents hoped would make the child understand their motives in placing; and the birthparents would be assured that their child was loved and safe. Although both adoptive parents and birthparents cited positive features of openness, some serious reservations were raised. Several of the adoptive parents felt that the ongoing relationship with the birthparent was intrusive or potentially threatening, and that they were uncomfortable with the birthparents' expressions of affection to their children and sadness at separating from them. Birthparents likewise expressed some reservations, primarily around issues concerning the continuing grief at the loss of the child. Some had resolved this by fantasizing that the child would come live with them later on, or by wanting to have active involvement in the rearing of their birthchildren.

The next two vignettes depict the Martin and Griffith families, both of whom had very positive experiences with fully disclosed adoptions. The third vignette, that of the Rowan family, illustrates some of the potential problems that may develop in very open adoptions. It should be reiterated that the children in this study were quite young, and it is still too early to determine the long-term consequences of openness on adopted children.

James and Connie Martin

Dr. and Mrs. Martin have two adopted children, Brett, aged five, and Melissa, aged three. Brett was adopted at the age of 24 months and Melissa was adopted at birth. Both adoptions are fully disclosed and the two birthmothers, as well as Brett's birth-grandmother, visit on a regular basis. Dr. James Martin, 42, is a university professor, and Mrs. Connie Martin, 39, is a librarian.

(Mrs. Martin speaking)
We had been married about eight years when we decided to consider adopting a child. We had consulted with fertility specialists for years, before we finally admitted that I was infertile and that we would not have any birthchildren. We both came from large families and had a strong desire to be parents, so we decided to consider adoption. For a year or so, I spent all my spare time researching various adoption agencies and trying to determine which one would be the best for us.

We decided to select Lutheran Social Service because it was the most flexible regarding lifestyle, religious faith, and age. As Jim was getting close to the upper age limit for many agencies, we were very pleased when the Lutheran agency agreed to work with us and did not seem to feel that his age was a problem. We first went to a meeting to learn more about the agency and the qualifications for adoptive parenthood. The agency representative said that they wanted families who would consider openness in their adoption. That didn't bother us, because only a week or so earlier, we had been talking about that very thing. We had seen a show on television about problems birthparents experience and we had said that agencies should really consider the needs of birthparents in adoptive placements. So, when LSST mentioned openness, we were enthusiastic.

We had a couple of interviews with our assigned worker and then we attended a day-and-a-half seminar that the agency sponsored. We talked a lot about the myths surrounding adoption and had a chance to talk about our own attitudes about adoption, birthparents, and were able to get rid of some stereotypes we had. The best part of the meeting was our visit with birthmothers. LSST brought in a panel of birthmothers to tell us how they felt about giving up their babies for adoption. We had a chance to talk with the mothers and, wow, did we learn from them. During that seminar, we also did a role play in which Jim had to play the role of a birthfather. I had to play the role of the adoptive mother who had to answer my child's questions about her birthmother. I had to come up with the best way to respond to the questions.

After the seminar, we had another couple of visits and individual interviews with our worker, filled out some forms, and had to write social histories on each of us. We knew that these social histories would be shared with birthmothers to assist them in their choice of adoptive parents for their babies.

Then the waiting began. Actually it wasn't as long as we thought it would be. We completed our study in November, and almost exactly four months later, we got the call. Sally, our worker, said that our little girl had been born on March 15 and that she wondered if we would like to be her parents. We were elated—I think I dropped the phone—I really don't remember—I just couldn't believe it. I called Jim at the office and said, "come home immediately." When I told him the news he just sat down and cried.

Our worker had told us that the birthmother, Jill, had wanted to meet us before she made her final decision to relinquish Melissa. Jill was about 24 years old when Melissa was born. She was from North Dakota and had moved to Texas to find a job. All of her relatives were deceased. Upon moving to Houston, she met a fellow and ended up getting pregnant. He left her to fend for herself. Jill was trying to make it on her own and knew there was no way she could raise a child also. She met another guy, Roy, whom she began to depend on for emotional support throughout the pregnancy. He told her that she should do what was best for her and the baby. Jill realized that raising a baby would jeopardize her future and that she really wanted the baby to have a good, solid, two-parent family.

When we came to the agency that day in March, Jill and her boyfriend, Roy, were both there to meet with us. She said that she had read our social histories and was most impressed by the fact that we seemed to have a good marriage and could give so much to a child. She also was pleased that we would be accepting of an open adoption. We liked her right away—she was so friendly and, in no time, we felt that we had known her for years. Jill was studying to be a legal assistant and she said that there was no way she could adequately provide for the baby. We knew how much she would like to have raised Melissa herself and we were so thankful that she had chosen us to be Melissa's parents. We told her that our house would always be open to her for visits with the baby. Melissa was placed with us two days later.

Circumstances were a little bit different with Brett's adoption. We had had Melissa for about six months, when we de-

cided that we really wanted another child. We knew that the
likelihood of our getting another would decrease as we became
older. Therefore, we decided to put our application in again.
We were invited to an intake meeting of reapplicants. At this
meeting we realized that the agency was now taking a stronger
stance on behalf of open adoptions. Since we were having a
successful open arrangement with Melissa and Jill, we were
asked to talk with the other reapplicants about our experience.
We were becoming real advocates for open adoptions.

Soon after we had completed the abbreviated reapplication
procedure, we received a call about Brett. We were told that
he was now two years old and had been living with his 19-
year-old birthmother and other relatives since his birth. They
were no longer able to take care of him and had decided to
place him for adoption. Brett's family wanted to be certain that
they could have ongoing contact with him so they insisted on a
family willing to have a fully disclosed adoption. I guess LSST
thought of us, since we were so pleased with our relationship
with Melissa's mother.

We met Brett and his birthmother, Amy, about a week later.
I could tell how very much she loved him and how difficult it
was for her to give him up. Amy was 17 when she became pregnant after her first sexual experience. Her boyfriend advised
her to have an abortion before he left town to get a job. She
completed high school while pregnant and relied on her divorced parents for support. After Brett's birth, she took care of
him at home for about six months. Then, she left him periodically with an elderly aunt while she attempted to find a job. As
he became older, and his needs increased, she realized that it
wasn't fair to him to try to keep him. So Amy first contacted
LSST and made adoption plans. However, on the day of the
placement Amy did not show—her aunt was there to present
Brett to us.

We were delighted that we had been chosen for Brett, but
there were times when we felt overwhelmed with two children
so young. Melissa took to Brett immediately and they have become very close. Since Brett was very attached to his birthmother, it was hard for him to adjust to us in the beginning.
At placement, we agreed that Brett would stay with us for about
six weeks before a visit would be arranged with Amy or her
aunt.

We now have two very different open adoptions, but I think

they are going great. Amy lives about 200 miles from us, but she comes to visit about once every two months. Her relatives live in town, and she relies on them to visit Brett when she is unavailable. In the beginning, she experienced a great deal of pain upon seeing Brett. She just couldn't leave him alone, and I could see that she was crying as she watched him play from a distance. It has been so hard on her—especially since she raised him for the first two years of his life. She and Brett love to play together—they romp in the backyard and he really enjoys playing catch with her.

Amy especially enjoys her freedom to take Brett with her away from our house. She frequently asks to take him to a movie. When she is in town, and we want to go somewhere, we get her to babysit both of the kids. She enjoys being with us in our house, but she seems to always plan to spend some time alone with him.

We are fairly close to Amy, but not nearly as close as we are to Melissa's birthmom, Jill. Amy is so much younger than we are and seems to march to a different drummer. She is very quiet and we really don't know what she is thinking. I'm sure she wishes she could have raised Brett herself, but she knows he is in a good home. She seems to like us. Only recently has she taken us up on our invitation to stay with us in our home when she visits Brett.

Some people tell us that we should not let Amy take Brett off by herself because they fear she will not return. Yes, of course, there are times when we feel anxious about this, but not very often. Amy knows Brett is happy with us. He began calling us Mommy and Daddy only a few weeks after he came to live with us. We didn't tell him to do that—he just did. He now calls his birthmother Amy.

I am glad that we know where his birthmother is, so we won't ever live in fear that she is hiding in some corner waiting to snatch him. We know what kind of person she is, and she knows what kind of persons we are. I know about her medical background, and if there is some other information I need to know, I can call her or some of her relatives.

The same thing is true with Jill, Melissa's birthmom. I know who she is, where she is, and the kind of person she is. She is now married to Roy, and they both come down frequently to visit us. She loves to make gifts for the children. Jill was absolutely delighted when we adopted Brett, because she had al-

ways hoped that Melissa would have a big brother. She loves
Brett like he was her own. She gets on the floor and plays with
them and buys presents for both of them. In fact, Jill and Amy
seem to love both of the kids and enjoy doing things with them.
   Brett and Melissa see Jill as a family friend. They love it
when we tell them that Jill and Roy are coming for a visit.
They help me bake cookies and plan dinner for them.
   We have discussed adoption with both of the kids and they
understand all about their origins. Brett and Melissa have been
told that my uterus didn't work, so they had to grow up in
someone else's uterus. They know that Jill and Amy are their
birthmoms, but I don't believe that they really know what the
term means. We think it is important that our children know
who their birthparents are and we are helping them understand this. It's also important for birthmothers to know where
their children are and to know that they haven't been killed or
injured. They need to have peace of mind that they are all right.
   Jill went through holy hell during the first few months after
placing Melissa. She still hurts inside, I'm sure, but her pain
is eased knowing that Melissa is happy and that she can see
her whenever she wants to. She and Roy plan to have children
of their own soon, and I am sure that they will continue to be
in touch with us. She always wanted Melissa to be in a stable
situation, and I know that she will never run off with her, because she doesn't want to mess up the family she created for
her. I have no problem with her deciding to take her to the
park, or anywhere else, because I know she will return her.
   It's almost like an extended family. When Melissa's birthmom, Roy, Amy, and her folks all come down, we have a ball.
Everyone loves the children, and they seem so happy to be together.

Jill Malone: Melissa Martin's Birthmother

Jill Malone, Melissa's birthmother, is now 27 years old and
married. She has a high school education and works as a legal
assistant. Jill lives about 100 miles away from the Martins
and visits every three or four months.

   (Jill Malone speaking)
   I had been on the pill and didn't even realize I was pregnant

until I was about four months along. Since I am Catholic, I wouldn't have considered abortion, even if I had known about my pregnancy earlier. When I told my boyfriend, he said he would not help me if I decided to raise the child. I knew I couldn't raise the baby alone, but I couldn't bear placing it for adoption and never seeing it again. I remembered that I had heard a person at church once speak about the open-adoption program sponsored through Lutheran Social Service. I thought that it might be worth a try to talk with a counselor there and see what they had to say.

I was surprised at how supportive the agency was. You know, I didn't have to place her if I didn't want to. The choice was totally up to me. There was no pressure at all. I didn't have to do anything. The only thing I didn't like was all the paper signing at the end. I knew all along that I wanted an open adoption—I wanted ongoing contact with my child. I think the secretive, closed approach is barbaric. Birthmothers must know that their children are all right. I have to be able to pick up the phone and check on her or just talk to her mother.

Before I had the baby, I told the worker that if I were to relinquish my child, I must meet the family, and that I wanted to present the baby to them myself. They agreed that that would be acceptable. When Melissa was born, I named her Reneé Louise in the hospital. I got to feed her and hold her each day I was there. I really wanted the adoptive family to be with me during labor and delivery, but that couldn't be arranged for some reason. I did get to meet the Martins when the baby was about three days old. I liked them immediately and decided that they would be the family for Reneé. I even liked the new name they gave her—Melissa. My best friend in high school had the same name.

I decided not to be present on placement day. We had exchanged names and addresses when we first met, but I wasn't sure if I would ever actually call them. One day, about a couple of weeks after her placement, I became very depressed. I called a friend, who encouraged me to pick up the phone and call the Martins to check on Melissa. I debated doing it for about an hour, and then finally I got up the nerve. Connie answered, and she was delighted to hear from me. We began to talk about Melissa, and she asked me all kinds of questions about my family's physical characteristics. We both predicted Melissa's hair color and size. I also told her about an orthopedic problem

I had had as a child and advised her to watch out for that with Melissa. Before long, we were just laughing like old friends. She knew I was concerned about Melissa, so she suggested that they bring her to see me. I cried.

I had not been there on placement day, and I wanted so much to see her. They came over to my apartment, and we took pictures. Since then, we visit once every two or three months. I always come on birthdays and Christmas.

I'm sort of like an aunt to Melissa, or like a friend that comes to visit any normal family. Although her adoptive mother, Connie, has made her aware that I am her birthmother, I don't think she knows what that means. One day, she came up to me and said, "I was born in your uterus." I know she doesn't understand that term. She calls me by my first name. I've never wished she would call me mom, because I know I am not her mom—Connie is.

I'm very close to the Martins, and we are like one big family. My own parents are now deceased, and I only have my husband, Roy, and the Martins. I intend to use Connie and James as resources when we have children. They are saving some of Melissa's baby things for me.

I have made Melissa quite a few little outfits and I hope one day that something I have given her will become her favorite thing. I want her to see me as a favorite aunt or close friend. I want her to feel free to ask me questions when she gets older.

The best thing about our placement is that I always know how Melissa is doing. Once I had this terrible dream that the Martins had divorced, and the agency had taken Melissa and Brett away from them. I woke up screaming and went right to the phone and called Connie. She assured me all was well and let me talk with both kids on the phone. I don't know what birthmothers do who can't call up and find out about their kids.

All of my visits with the Martins have occurred at their home. I think she is too young for me to take her out of her environment now. Later on, when she's older, I may want to take her with me somewhere or to spend a night at my home. It will all depend on whether she wants to, and if the Martins think it is a good idea. I know that Melissa is just where Melissa needs to be—with the Martins. She belongs with them.

I was so excited when Connie and James adopted Brett—I always wanted Melissa to have a brother. I love all four of them so much. They are a perfect family.

Amy Jarrett: Brett Martin's Birthmother

Amy Jarrett, Brett's birthmother, was 16 years old when Brett was born. She is now 21 years old and works part-time as a sales clerk. Amy is Catholic and lives about 200 miles from the Martins.

(Amy Jarrett speaking)

When I got pregnant, I was only 16 years old. My boyfriend refused to get married and even denied that Brett was his child. I felt that Brett deserved to have a two-parent family, but that I would try to raise him myself. While I was pregnant, I had inquired about adoption, but I never actually went in to talk with a counselor at an agency.

After his birth, I stayed at home with him for a while. Then I got a couple of jobs to help support him and eventually had to leave him with my aunt. My mother would have kept him, but she worked too. As he got older, it became too difficult for my aunt to keep up with him. I then started leaving him at a child-care center. He sometimes had to stay at night, if I had to work a night shift.

My parents were divorced and my father didn't want to have anything to do with me or the baby. When Brett was about two, I realized that I could no longer handle him. I contacted an attorney to arrange an adoption. When I told my aunt what I had done, she suggested that I contact an adoption agency. She said she had heard an ad about an agency that let the birthmother keep in contact with the child. I recalled that, when I was pregnant, I had heard about that program, and decided to check around to get the name of the agency. The people were really nice at Lutheran Social Service and seemed to understand what a difficult decision I was having to make.

They reassured me that Brett would go to a good family and that I could keep in touch with him. My out-of-state relatives couldn't understand why I would let my baby be adopted, but my close friends and family knew I couldn't handle him by myself. As long as I could keep in contact, I felt it would be OK.

The agency gave me letters from parents who were wanting to adopt and I saw the options I had for how open each family wanted to be. I read the Martins' letter and felt really comfortable with it. They indicated that they already had a little girl and wanted another child. They seemed very warm.

Before the placement, I met Connie and James. I already
knew that I would probably pick them for Brett, and I found
that I liked them right away. But it was too difficult for me to
be there on placement day. I signed the papers, but my aunt
actually gave him to the Martins on placement day. A couple
of months passed before I saw him again.

Until then, he had always called me mom, but the next time
I saw him, he called Connie "mom." He remembered me, but
he called me Amy. At first that bothered me, but now I'm comfortable with it. If he wants to call me mom when he's older,
that's OK.

They have really been good to him. He is such a friendly
little guy. He knows I am a friend of the family—he doesn't
really understand that I am his mom. I love to be with him
and feel most comfortable with him when I take him away from
home.

I keep telling him that when he turns 18 or 19, I'll still be in
my 30s, and we'll go out and drink a beer and go dancing. If he
reaches his teen years and decides he'd prefer to come live with
me, I would welcome it. However, if the Martins said no, I would
go along with their wishes.

I do miss him. He is such a great little guy. When he comes
up and hugs me, I like that. It doesn't happen every day so
you've got to cherish the ones that you do get. Since I live some
distance from him, my mom or my aunt visit the Martins frequently. They feel very welcome in their home.

I know he's happy where he is and I know he loves the Martins. I will always be a part of his life, though. He thinks of me
as a friend, and I think of the Martins as friends. One day I
hope we will all be like relatives.

Thomas and Karen Griffith

Thomas and Karen Griffith are well educated, and highly
motivated parents. Thomas, now in his late 40s, is an attorney in private practice. Karen, in her late 30s, is an adminis-
trator with a master's degree. They have three children: Julie,
aged six, their first adopted daughter; Sandy, aged five, their
second adopted daughter; and Jason, their son by birth, aged
15 months. Julie and Sandy were both placed with the Griffiths immediately after birth. Thomas and Karen strongly

wanted a family, although Karen experienced difficulty in getting pregnant and then had a miscarriage. When Thomas approached the upper age limit for adopting, they decided that they would enter into the adoption process.

(Mrs. Griffith speaking)
We thought we had a pretty good idea of what to expect in the adoption process, because we researched it quite a bit. The initial screening was a bit intimidating, however, because you were in a room with 50 other couples who wanted to adopt, and you knew that somehow you had to convince the agency people in five minutes or less that you were more capable than at least 40 of the others. After we got our initial approval that we had been selected for further study, we had to attend seminars, get letters of recommendation, obtain certification of infertility, and fill out a lot of paperwork—basically, we had to spill our guts.

We were always wondering if we were going to say the wrong thing or do something that might jeopardize our chances—and the other couples had the same fear. During the time when you're waiting for your child, or you've just had a child placed with you and you still have six months to go through, you're probably going to go along with anything the agency suggests. I don't think we would have said "no" to anything because we wanted a family so desperately.

For our first child, we wanted a newborn, but had no sex preferences. When we adopted Julie, the agency wasn't doing face-to-face meetings yet. However, when she was six months old, her birthmother, Linda, contacted the agency to find out how she was and to see if we would be willing to send a picture of her. It seemed pretty foreign to send pictures and letters, because our attitude was still the traditional one, that the birthmother was the person out there that might try to snatch our child back. We decided that we were happy to exchange letters or pictures through the agency, but we weren't ready for direct communication. In the first picture we sent, Julie was way off in the distance so that she really couldn't be identified in a crowd. However, some of the workshops and seminars put on by the agency began to change our minds about openness.

We first met Linda when Julie was three and a half years' old. (It was actually after we had met Sandy's birthmom). We met at the agency, and we were all scared. Immediately there was a sense of bonding, because we had this child that we all loved. There was a lot of love and a lot of crying; it was very emotional. We have continued to have some sporadic contact with Linda. When she was planning to get married, she invited me to her wedding shower. Although she lives about 300 miles from here, she still calls now and then. We've invited her to come for a visit, but she hasn't taken us up on it yet.

We've told Julie about her birthmother and that she grew inside her tummy instead of mine. We have shown her the pictures from our meeting with her, and she includes Linda in her prayers every night. I keep offering to talk with Julie about adoption. I feel totally prepared. But at her age, as soon as we begin a conversation, she's off doing something else.

The funny thing is that, if it were up to us, Julie would probably have more contact with Linda. However, since it's left up to Linda, she doesn't seem to need it or want it right now. It's ironic.

Sandy's story turned out differently. We met her birthmother, Nancy, after exchanging letters for several years and finally revealing our names to one another. She was very interested in maintaining contact and wanted an open relationship, which was fine with us by that time. When she was dating the young man whom she later married, he seemed very accepting of her relationship with Sandy. However, after they were married, he insisted that she choose between her marriage or her relationship with us and Sandy. She wrote and said that she wouldn't be able to contact us anymore, which I think is sad for everybody. I thought, "How could she reject us? If she could only see Sandy, there's no way she could do that." I will continue to send the people at the agency pictures and letters, in case later she wants to check in.

I doubt that Linda and Nancy will have very large roles in our daughters' lives. Maybe when they are 20, the children will want to find them. And my fantasy is that our whole family will work together to find them. I know that there will be tough times, when the girls ask, "Why did my birthmother give me up, or give me away?", or whatever words they use. Maybe we've dealt with it so well by now that it won't be an issue, but we'll see.

We're really happy with the openness in our adoption. It has worked well for us, although the bottom line is that it isn't necessarily the best for everybody.

Linda Jones: Julie Griffith's Birthmother

Linda was 19 when she became pregnant by Frank, who was 17 and still in high school. They didn't want to get married, and adoption seemed like the only choice.

(Linda Jones speaking)
When I found out that I was pregnant, I looked in the yellow pages to find a doctor. It just happened that the doctor I called put me in touch with a lawyer who was connected with the adoption agency. It was God's will that it worked out that way because, like I say, I just got him out of the phone book.

I didn't find out I was pregnant until four months before Julie was born. My family insisted that I give the baby up. At that time, I didn't have any confidence in myself, so I felt I had better not buck the system, since they would support me only if I gave up the baby. Even though it was hard then, I could hug them all now for pushing it. My father and I never talked about it very much. In his mind, it never happened. Even though I live just a few blocks from him now, we never talk about it. He doesn't want to hear it.

When I was in the hospital to deliver, they put me out so that I would not see the baby. After she was born, they even moved me to another floor in the hospital so that I wouldn't be with all the new mothers and babies. It was OK until a nurse's aide came in one evening and told me that she heard that I had just given my baby up for adoption and she couldn't believe that I had done it. That put me into orbit. Before I went home, I did go down and hold her for about 30 minutes, and then that was the last I saw of her.

I didn't receive any counseling either before or after my pregnancy. I just kept it all inside for two years. I wrote letters to her adoptive parents through the agency and asked for pictures, but I could tell that they were nervous. I was worried that they didn't love her. But since we met each other, I have never worried about her. They have given her a lot more than I ever could. I've been to their house, and I feel very good about her situation. I don't look at her as my daughter. She is their child.

My husband hasn't met Julie yet. It's kind of hard for him, because he would have wanted my first child to be ours. In the future, I will have my own life. I won't exclude Julie, but she'll never think of me as anything but a friend. I hope we'll be close as adults too.

Paul and Sharon Rowan

Paul and Sharon Rowan, aged 34 and 32, respectively, are the adoptive parents of two children: Danny, aged five, and Tina, aged three and a half. Danny was placed with the Rowans when he was three years' old; Tina was placed at the age of two days.

(Mrs. Rowan speaking)

We really wanted a family, but were unable to have children of our own, after having tried for six years. We initially petitioned to adopt through an agency that does international placements. However, we needed a local adoption agency to do our home study, and we liked the caseworkers so much that we decided to try our luck with them. It took us about one and a half years from the time we began the adoption process until we actually got Tina. We expected the adoption process to be long and hard. There were ups and downs. The hardest part was the waiting. By the time we finally were approved, it only took a few months for Tina to be placed with us.

We were never really offered a closed adoption, but we could limit it to certain things we were comfortable with. You could have face-to-face meetings, or you could just write letters and exchange pictures. We had no idea that it would be as ongoing as it has been. It has really turned out to be just what we wanted, but the relationship with Tina's birthmother is a lot easier than with Danny's birthparents.

When we found out that Tina was born, we took a risk and went to the hospital before Ann (Tina's birthmother) signed the papers. Although we knew she might change her mind, we went ahead and took the chance. We were scared to death to meet her. We knew she'd be nervous and that she hadn't made up her mind about what to do yet. Our case worker went in the hospital room with us, but then she left after a few minutes. It worked real well. We had been coached a little about what to expect. Our worker suggested that we get Ann a little gift and to just act natural. We could tell that she had been crying a lot. She looked like she'd been going through a lot of pain and stress, but we talked, and then they went to get the baby. Ann held her, and we all looked at her together and counted her toes and talked about how pretty she was. We took a few pictures, and Ann showed us some pictures of her family. She gave Tina a little stuffed bear that played a tune. I had to be real strong not to start crying. When she gave us the bear, we felt that she was probably going to go through with the placement. We did get to feed Tina a little in the room, and a real strong bond formed between us and Ann during that short meeting. If she ever called and said she needed us or needed help, we'd be right there. We felt sad for her, giving up Tina. The next morning we went to the hospital to pick up the baby, and Ann had already checked out. She went to Oregon to visit her parents, and we didn't see her for another year. Her mother wrote to us a few times to see how the baby was. She tried to get Ann to write us, but she just couldn't yet. So we sent pictures and wrote to her mom.

We didn't see Ann again until we met her, entirely by chance, at a shopping mall about a year later. We were there with Tina in a baby stroller, and I turned to Paul and said, "I can't believe it, but I think that's Ann." We went over to her and arranged to get together the following week. It was hard for her at first. She kept talking about how much older Tina was. She said that she left a little baby, but now Tina's a girl. It wasn't the same child she left us. But every meeting was a little easier. And now we are really close to her. Ann got married not too long ago, and her husband was transferred to Florida. We don't see her too often, but we still keep in touch.

Danny's situation was very different. Danny's parents, Pat and Mark, were both in their late 20s when they decided to get a divorce. Pat was very career-minded, and Mark worked as a traveling salesman. From what we can tell, Danny was in daycare, full time, at least six days each week. Both Pat and Mark wanted Danny to have two parents, so they decided to place him. It seemed especially sad, though, because Mark was just told one day to come down and sign the papers. He had probably agreed to place his son, but it didn't really hit him until he had to sign. I just remembered how sad he looked. We could tell that he and his son were very close.

We seemed to have many tests to pass before we got Danny. Pat kept grilling us about our family, our jobs, our income, and how we would raise Danny. It was like Danny was on the other side of a brick wall, and we had better break through it, or we'd never get him. Mark was just sad to lose his son. We had to tell both of them that we didn't want to steal their son. If they wanted to keep him, they should. We went through one week when the agency would call and say it looks like she's going to sign, and the next day they'd call and say that it doesn't look like she's going to sign. So we were up and down every day. But they finally decided that adoption was the best for Danny.

We don't see Pat very often, because she's moved to another town. But Mark is over here all the time. Paul considers him like a brother. Open adoption is good in that it lets Danny know that Pat and Mark haven't abandoned him. He's living with "mom and dad" at home, but he knows that they still love him.

I'll never forget the first time Danny saw Mark after he came to us. They just lay in each other's arms for about 30 minutes and didn't say a word. It was like Danny's little world had just come to an end. He's really attached to Mark. Even though it's great that Danny gets to see his birthparents, it can get a bit crazy around here. Sometimes a week will go by when nothing happens, and then there will be a time when you really get emotionally worn out because you really have to prepare for the visits. Sometimes we really have to put our foot down and say that we had planned a certain family event and we just can't change our plans. And it's not only Mark. Danny has several aunts and uncles and his grandparents who come over, too. So it's like we inherited a huge extended family when we adopted him. You have to be careful what you say around whom. You can't really agree or disagree with people, because one might get the word back to someone else.

We don't see Pat too often now, but there was a time when she was really pressuring us. She'd call us all the time or cut down Mark. Finally, I just had to tell her that she didn't have to worry about what was going on, and that we will decide when she will see Danny. Then she started to pressure us again after I'd already set the rules. So we had to say "no" and set the rules again. She has backed off a little now.

I feel a little sorry for Tina, because her birthfather is on the run. She sees Danny's relatives over here all the time, and she's going to wonder why her birthfather is never around. We have talked to him on the phone and sent him pictures, but he said the pictures hurt him. We've left the door open with him, but now our contact is going through the agency. Maybe he will come around on his own time.

Mark has a girlfriend now and is planning to get married. She's a little assertive and now tries to make the arrangements for visits. I don't know how far to trust her. She gets down on the floor and plays with the kids, but I think she's trying to go too fast. If his girlfriend weren't there, I'd feel more comfortable with Mark. I think she's using her relationship with the kids to get closer to Mark. She's the outsider in our program now. She's pushy, and we've been pushed enough.

There's a little rivalry between Paul and Mark over Danny. They're both saving a special rifle for him. I told him, you'd just better put your foot down. I've talked to Mark and asked him what's going to happen if Danny decides he wants to go back and live with him. Mark said he wouldn't let him, and I said that was good because I wouldn't let him either!

Our contact with the agency is so important. We just can't run off and leave the agency, because we're running into special problems that "normal" families don't have. You can't just adopt and leave. You have to have someone to fall back on.

Ann Webber: Tina Rowan's Birthmother

Ann Webber was 20 years old when Tina was born. After placing Tina immediately after her birth, Ann moved away, but later reestablished contact with the Rowans. Although she has remarried and now lives in Florida, she still keeps in contact.

(Ann Webber speaking)

Steve and I were going together, but we broke up before I knew that I was pregnant. I didn't even tell him about the baby until three weeks after placement. I was staying with a girlfriend of mine, had no job, no place of my own, so I decided I couldn't raise this baby. I certainly didn't want to go on welfare. I looked in the phone book and found only one adoption agency in town. I did want openness; I would have kept the baby if I couldn't keep in touch with how she was doing.

When I was working with the agency, I read letters from 15 different couples who wanted to adopt. There were only two that were willing to have some degree of openness. I never dreamed that we would become this close, but I feel that they are "OK people" now.

I first met the Rowans in the hospital. I had no idea of what to expect. But when I saw them holding her, I knew that they all looked happy and that it would work out. At first, I felt terrible. I cried every day. I didn't feel really good until a year later. Just by chance, I ran into them in the shopping mall. It was so strange, because I had kept fantasizing about this baby that I left. But now she was a girl! I realized that Tina was their girl now, not my baby anymore.

Mark Robins: Danny Rowan's Birthfather

Mark Robins is a 32-year old construction worker, currently divorced, but planning to remarry in the near future. He visits his son regularly at the home of the Rowans.

(Mark Robins speaking)

Pat and I were divorced soon after Danny was born. He lived with her, but I stayed in close touch. I would pick him up every day and take him to day-care. When we decided to place Danny, I told the social worker that I did want to meet his adoptive parents. After meeting once at the agency, we just decided that we would stay in touch with each other directly.

I feel great about my relationship with Paul and Sharon. I think being able to see Danny has had a positive effect. I think he's a lot happier about it, and I know I am. I walk away from visits feeling good that he's doing so well.

Danny calls me Mark now. Of course, before the adoption, he called me daddy. At first, he continued to call me daddy, and then about six months ago he changed. It was hard to get used to at first. I wish he would still call me dad.

There are times when I still wish that he was mine. I'd like to raise him. I still see him as my son. In my mind, I'm always going to be there for him. Even my family still says, "He still has a son."

The hardest part of the relationship is having to leave after visits. But we've gone from strangers to friends to almost family. I'm going to get married in about six months, and I want to keep up the contact with Danny. We're going to bring him up knowing that he can't just hop from house to house anytime he feels like it. But as far as his making a rational decision to live with us once he's old enough to make a rational decision, we'd have to deal with that when it comes up. I realize that when I signed that paper I pretty much relinquished all my rights. Paul and Sharon have given me a lot more than they really have to give me.

COMPARISONS

In comparing the responses given by families in the three groups, a striking similarity is that each set of parents felt that their type of adoption was the best situation. It is likely that this preference is due to the type of preparation offered by the agency before adoption. (See Chapter 4 for further discussion of this point). In addition, each family was very complimentary of the agency's role in their adoption.

Adoptive families in confidential and semiopen adoptions shared a view of the birthmother that involved both fear (of her reclaiming the child or of being a pest if ongoing contact were occurring) and a negative stereotype. Both sets of adoptive parents seemed pleased to be insulated from having a relationship with the birthparents. Adoptive parents in fully disclosed situations did not actively express fear of the child's being reclaimed; in fact, they felt that they had control over the relationship with the birthparents. The negative factors for them were the inconvenience and the effort involved in working on the relationship with the birthparents (as in the Rowan family) and their discomfort at seeing the birthparent's pain on an ongoing basis. In addition, some expressed an interest in lessening the degree of openness in the relationship, but were concerned about hurting the birthparent's feelings. Some open adoptive parents (e.g., the Martins and Griffiths) expressed a very positive attitude toward the relationship.

Birthmothers in the semiopen adoptions wanted more information and felt cut off from their children, even though they had pictures and maintained correspondence with the adoptive family through the agency. However, the same general theme was also present with the birthparents in the fully disclosed adoptions: even though they had ongoing contact with their children, they expressed the desire to be fuller parents. Several actively expressed a hope that the child would eventually live with them. Unlike the birthmothers in the semiopen situations, the birthmothers in the fully disclosed group often felt close to their adoptive families and felt as if they were a member of the family. Although the role that they named was as an "aunt" or a "friend," the interviews and observations of the researchers suggested that the birthmothers were more like older daughters of their adoptive parents. They sought advice from their child's adoptive parents and often relied on them for emotional support (as in the Martin family).

In summary, analysis of the interviews with adoptive parents and birthparents suggests the following conclusions. The confidential adoption situation appears to allow the adoptive parents to take full parenting responsibility for their children and to deal as much or as little with adoption issues as they wish. Depending on the parents, this situation might permit adoptive parents to deny the difference between adoptive and biological parenting and to restrict communication with the child about his or her adoptive status and heritage. Some concern is expressed for the child's right to know about his or her birthparents, but the adoptive parents will likely not encourage the child's searching unless the child presses for it. If the adoptive parents are secretive or noncommunicative with the child, identity issues in adolescence may present challenges for the entire family. In the confidential situation, the birthparent loses all contact with the child and all information about the child.

Semiopen adoptions provide benefits to all parties in the adoption triad. The adoptive parents are insulated from interference in their lives with the child; but at the same time, they are in contact with the birthparent(s) and facilitate a communication link between birthparent and child. The birthparents in semiopen adoptions benefit by having the information that they appear to want the most: the knowledge that the child is in a loving environment and is happy and healthy. Although the birthparents may desire more information about the child, a more open situation is not necessarily less painful for them. In fact, ongoing contact appeared to be very stressful for a number of the birthmothers interviewed in this study. The children benefit in that they have avenues for communication with their birthparents and have knowledge about their heritage. Depending on the specific individuals involved, the door may be open for contact between children and birthparents when the children are of legal age.

Fully disclosed adoptions involving ongoing contact appear to benefit the children and the birthparents more than the adoptive parents. The children have the love and attention of another adult and come to know the birthparent as a real (as opposed to a fantasized) person. The birthparent has access to the child and can watch him or her grow up. This situation evokes mixed emotions: It is reassuring to know that the child is happy and well taken care of; however, it is also painful to see your child and know that you cannot have him or her. In some cases, ongoing contact seemed to encourage the birthparent's fantasy that the child might return to live with them. The benefits to the adoptive parents seem somewhat less clear. The greatest benefit is that it gives them a realistic picture of the birthparent and prevents stereotyping. At the same time, however, several of the adoptive parents became parents not only to the child, but also to the birthparent. Some of them were concerned about having to meet the emotional needs expressed by their children's birthparents and were uncomfortable with the birthparents' intrusiveness.

The boundaries of families experiencing fully disclosed openness are constantly open to change. Since no formal rules exist to guide the behavior of the members of the adoption triad, roles must be negotiated on an ongoing basis. Adoptive parents must be ready and willing to accept the challenges involved with engaging a whole new network of individuals. Most of the families experiencing fully disclosed openness in this study have coped well with the demands of this situation. However, their children are still young and many new and unknown challenges await these pioneers.

7

Values and Risks of Openness in Adoption

In 1981, the Children's Home Society of Minnesota (CHSM) prepared a report on their Openness in Adoption Pilot Project, which listed a number of values and risks of openness to all members of the adoption triad. Those values and risks are listed in this chapter, and the validity of each one is discussed in light of the data collected in this research project. The statements below that are italicized are those of the Children's Home Society. It is important to note that CHSM defined openness as follows: *Having a meeting or live contact, face-to-face, video-tape, via telephone, etc., between birthparents who have terminated parental rights and potential adoptive parents without the sharing of identifying information. Such meeting or contact will be arranged and monitored by the agency.*

BIRTHPARENTS

Values

1. *Increased openness in adoption procedures can create greater feelings of remaining in control over their decision by*

making them partners in the adoption process. A contact, personal meeting, telephone call, or written contact might allay residual anxiety about the child's future and remove fantasies about the child's living situation. Comments of birthparents interviewed in this study strongly support this statement as a value of openness. An overriding interest of all birthparents was the need to be assured about their child's well-being.

2. *The proposed increased openness in adoption would allow birthparents to live more comfortably with their decision, as they would not send the child into the unknown.* This value was strongly supported by the data collected in this study. Several birthparents commented that they would never have placed their child unless it had been in a situation that permitted openness.

3. *There would be less secrecy, less of a perceived sense of punitive separation. This may reduce the sense of guilt and shame and relieve the need to find the child later on.* Although birthparents did not typically note feelings of guilt or shame, they nevertheless did express interest in greater contact with the child as he or she matured. Some birthparents fantasized that the child would eventually live with them. We cannot conclude that reduced guilt would relieve the need for contact with the child. In fact, the situation may work in reverse: birthparents who have resolved their feelings of guilt may feel more worthy of and entitled to contact.

Risks

1. *Rejection of the birthparents by the adoptive parents, or vice versa, for whatever reason, would be difficult for both parties.* There is no doubt that rejection would be difficult. However, all adoptive parents and birthparents received careful and thorough preparation for their initial contact and were prepared to meet each other in an accepting manner. It should go without saying that careful preparation and supervision will continue to be essential components of open-adoption placements.

2. *Ambivalence of the birthparent(s) toward the adoptive parents might result in an ongoing emotional burden for the*

birthparent(s). Although this could be true, the birthparents interviewed in this study typically expressed satisfaction and gratitude toward their child's adoptive parents. This may be due to the birthparents' participation in the selection of the child's adoptive parents.

3. *Feelings of regret about their decision or jealousy toward the adoptive parents might arise following a positive meeting in which a sense of closeness and intimacy develops.* Some of the birthparents interviewed did express regrets about their decision to place, expressed the wish to have the child back, and fantasized about future contact with the child. This finding emphasizes the need for continuing agency supervision in cases involving ongoing contact.

CHILD

Values

1. *A link with birthparents provided by adoptive parents may enhance a sense of life continuity, personal history, and self-worth.* Past research and the clinical work cited in Chapters 1 and 2 strongly suggest the value of this link. However, as the children in the current study were too young to be interviewed, our data cannot support or disconfirm this statement.

2. *The adoptive parents can assist their child to form a positive mental image of his/her birthparent(s) as responsible person(s) who cared for the child and thoughtfully transferred parenting.* Reality-based knowledge can undoubtedly assist the adoptive parents in conveying an accurate picture of the child's birthparent(s) to him or her. At the same time, it may make problematic situations (incest, drug use, prostitution, etc.) more difficult to convey to the child.

3. *The child may be less burdened by secrecy and less likely to feel abandoned, rejected, or "snatched away."* This may be true; however, it is clear that the birthparents of the children we interviewed will be going on with their own lives, marrying, and having children of their own. It may be very difficult for an adopted child to accept that he or she was placed, but subsequent children were "kept."

4. *The wish to search out and meet birthparent(s) might be strengthened.*

5. *The wish not to search out and meet birthparent(s) might be strengthened.* We are unable to address these issues directly, because the adopted children in the study were not old enough to be interviewed. We presume that the value of searching for and meeting one's birthparents would vary from case to case.

Risks

1. *Fear that the birthparent(s) might change their decision and wish to reclaim him/her may be created.* Although some birthparents did express interest in reclaiming their children, all did acknowledge that the adoption was legal and final. Similarly, some adoptive parents also expressed this concern while acknowledging the finality of the adoption. Some of the birthparents talked about the child's coming to live with them once the child was of age. Since the children themselves were not interviewed, we are unable to assess the impact of this risk on the child.

2. *Adoptive parents may report unsympathetically their impression of the birthparent(s) or resent and repress the reality of the birthparent(s).* No evidence was found to support this statement. In general, adoptive parents did not report negative impressions of birthparents.

3. *The child could misinterpret information leading to a heightened sense of rejection or fantasies denying present reality.* We are unable to address this concern, as the children in the study are still quite young and were not personally interviewed.

4. *A diminished quality of parent-child relationship may develop.* No evidence was found to support this statement, but the children in the study are still quite young and were not personally interviewed.

5. *The wish to search out and meet birthparent(s) might be strengthened.*

6. *The wish not to search out and meet birthparent(s) might be strengthened.* We are unable to address these issues di-

rectly because the adopted children in the study were not old enough to be interviewed. We presume that the value of searching for and meeting one's birthparents would vary from case to case.

ADOPTIVE PARENTS

Values

1. *Openness may help adoptive parents live more honestly with the reality of adoption and the child's origin. It allows less opportunity for fantasy regarding the child's origins and less opportunity for denial of infertility.* Kirk's theory of adoptive kinship is especially supportive of this conclusion. In general, much more denial of adoption was seen in the confidential cases interviewed, than in the semiopen or fully disclosed adoption cases.

2. *Information regarding the child's background/heritage can be communicated more realistically.* In general, this conclusion appears to be warranted. Adoptive parents in open situations have much more accurate and complete information about birthparents than do parents in confidential adoptions.

3. *A positive impression of the child's birthparent(s) can be conveyed and later communicated to the child.* Open adoption promotes communication of *accurate* information to the child, but that does not necessarily imply that the information is *positive.*

Risks

1. *The possibility of openness in adoption may subtly co-opt parents into a commitment they cannot keep because of the additional anxiety it will bring them in the future.* Some adoptive families in the fully disclosed group did express a desire to decrease the amount of openness in their relationship with the birthparent(s). However, they felt reluctant to request such a change because it might hurt the birthparent's feelings. Although they did not express this concern directly, they may

have also been concerned about jeopardizing any future adoption they may wish to transact with the agency. Changes in commitments seemed more related to the time involved than to increased anxiety.

2. *Anxiety caused by an effort to impress the birthparent(s) might introduce strain and an artificial quality to the contact.* Many of the open adoption families experiencing ongoing contact noted the stress of preparing for birthparent visits and the additional effort involved in maintaining the relationship. In general, they wanted to create a good impression on the birthparents and entertain them when they visited.

3. *A contact with birthparent(s) might increase feelings of inadequacy/guilt/shame related to infertility, followed by jealousy and anger toward birthparent(s).* No evidence in support of this statement emerged in the interviews. Adoptive parents in general did not speak much about their feelings concerning infertility.

4. *Negative impressions of the birthparent(s) might be passed on to the child.* Open adoption promotes accuracy in conveying impressions to the child, which may be either positive or negative. In general, most adoptive parents reported a positive impression of their children's birthparents.

5. *A possible negative initial impression might lead to a negative attitude toward the child's need to make contact with the birthparent(s) upon reaching maturity.* Although this generalization may be true, all adoptive parents in this study had positive impressions of their children's birthparents.

6. *Fears of birthparent(s)' interference in the form of recognition, intrusion, or lawsuit might be strengthened.* The strongest fears of birthparents' intrusion were found in the families with confidential adoptions; the least fear of the child being reclaimed was found in the cases of fully disclosed openness involving ongoing contact.

7. *A combination of some or all of the above might result in a diminished quality of bonding in the parent-child relationship.* This conclusion may be true; however, but it is premature to accept this statement on the basis of this study, because the children are still very young.

8

Practice Issues for Adoption Agencies

Agencies that choose to offer differing degrees of openness to their adoptive and birth family clients must also be aware of the practice implications of such a policy. Fully disclosed adoptions in particular have a lifelong impact on all members of the adoption triad, as well as the adoption agency.

During the adoption preparation process, adoption workers must be able to critically assess what, if any, degree of openness a family can handle. Similarly, birthparents must be screened to determine which form of openness would be most beneficial to them. As most agencies offering openness are more likely to use the group process adoption study procedure than traditional adoption agencies, it may be necessary to reassess whether workers are really able to evaluate the prospective adoptive couple accurately, using the group procedure primarily. Since some families are able to handle open adoptions easier than others, it may be necessary to develop very specific assessment tools and procedures to evaluate their readiness for openness. There may be some instances in which a casework assessment process would be advantageous. We feel strongly that the decision about the degree of openness should be made on a case-by-case basis.

FULLY DISCLOSED ADOPTIONS

In most cases of fully disclosed adoptions, the decision to reveal identifying information is made solely by birthparents and adoptive parents. Even in agencies in which identifying information is shared by the adoption agency at the time of adoption, agency personnel are only involved in the initial meetings. Arrangements for later meetings are often made independent of the agency. In many instances, the agency may not even be aware that an adoption that began with no exchange of identifying information may have become a fully disclosed adoption, with ongoing contact between all parties.

Since agencies may have minimal or no involvement at the time when many of the families choose to fully disclose, it is critical that they prepare and educate their adoptive and birth families, prior to the adoption, about the pros and cons of full disclosure. They must be aware that, as of this date, there is no research evidence to either support or reject open practices. The impact of ongoing contact on the child is still unknown. Moreover, they should be fully informed about the findings of this study, which illustrate some of the problems and issues with each type of adoption.

Many families, when choosing to fully disclose, fail to consider the future implications of such a decision. Some of the fully disclosed families in this study stated that they have a great deal of anxiety about the future. Many may wish to reduce the degree of openness in the relationship as the child matures, but fear that the birthparent may object or may be hurt.

Similarly, birthparents must be prepared to deal with some of the feelings they may experience upon regularly seeing their birthchild, who now legally belongs to another family. Many of the birthparents in this study expressed some guilt about relinquishing the child and regret that they could not raise their child. Several wished to reclaim the child, and others expressed the desire that the child might come to live with them during his or her adolescent years. Counseling services are needed to help them resolve some of these concerns and better accept the role that they now play in their child's life.

Postadoption counseling services must be offered to both adoptive and birth families to help them cope with the problems that may emerge and develop in a situation of fully disclosed adoption. Adoptive parents must be helped to deal with their feelings about setting limits and maintaining control over the involvement of birthparents in their children's lives. Staff may need to be trained in family counseling techniques, because there may be instances in which birthparents who have ongoing contact with the adoptive family and adoptee will need to meet together as a group to resolve problems in role expectations, family boundary disputes, and other troublesome issues. In addition, counseling may be needed to help the adoptee sort out the roles and relationships among adoptive parents and birthparents. These services should all be a part of the agency's postadoption program.

Agencies should offer a group counseling program in which adoptive parents and birthparents who have chosen a fully disclosed adoption have an opportunity to meet together, as well as with other families considering this option. The risks, as well as the benefits, should be considered. In many instances, having a fully disclosed adoption means that, not only is there ongoing contact with the birthmother, but with her extended family as well. Moreover, as noted in this study, many of the adoptive families have found that they have assumed parental roles, not only with the adopted child, but also with the birthparent. Families should be prepared for all these possibilities prior to their making a commitment to having a fully disclosed adoption.

Until there are sufficient longitudinal research data on the impact of ongoing contact on the adopted child, agencies may wish to develop guidelines for open adoptions, which are in keeping with the child's cognitive developmental level. Families should be advised as to what kind of contact, if any, they might consider between their adopted child and birthparents, depending on the child's developmental stage.

Group and individual counseling services should also be available to adopted children placed in open situations. These children will need help in dealing with their feelings about being adopted, as well as possible concerns about divided loyalties that may emerge through frequent contact with birth-parents and adoptive parents.

Agency supervisors may find that they must assume new roles as a result of the establishment of open adoptions. Because of the experimental nature of such programs at this time, supervisors will most likely have to increase supervisory time, in order to oversee these innovative practices. Moreover, supervisors may choose to keep a case load as well, in order to increase their awareness of direct service needs.

Administrators should assist staff and supervisors to determine who is the primary client of the agency. Agencies often claim to be child-oriented, but in reality are oriented toward either the adoptive parents or birthparents. If the best interests of the child are considered, agencies must recognize the need for ongoing services to adopted children who are involved in innovative adoption practices. In addition, specific fee structures will have to be established for all of these additional counseling services.

Therefore, before instituting any open-adoptions policy, agencies need to be apprised of the implications not only for the adoption triad, but also for the agency. Preadoption counseling services must be expanded to include discussions of openness, and agencies must develop a postadoption counseling-service division as a permanent part of their program. Agency administrators must also assess their staff's readiness for such a change, as well as the fiscal considerations of this innovation, in adoption practice.

SEMIOPEN ADOPTION

When offering semiopen adoptions, the agency makes a commitment to serve as intermediary between birthparents and adoptive parents for life, since information, pictures, gifts, and letters are typically exchanged through the agency. For some workers, this postadoption responsibility is added to their existing preadoptive parent preparation or birthparent counseling. This expanded caseload may produce stress for workers. In addition, workers need to be trained to serve as intermediaries, should adoptive families wish to increase or decrease the degree of openness in the adoption as the child gets older.

Since the worker is generally involved with clients before and after the adoption, a close relationship will probably exist between each client and his or her worker. If the worker should leave the agency, the client may feel abandoned, especially in a semiopen adoption situation in which the worker was the go-between. Agencies should be prepared to help their clients make the necessary transition, should their worker leave the agency.

Agencies must also take into account the additional costs involved with administering semiopen adoptions. Ongoing correspondence between adoptive families and birthparents as well as additional long distance phone calls can be expensive.

CONFIDENTIAL ADOPTIONS

As open-adoption practices become more and more popular, adoption agencies specializing in confidential adoptions will continually need to assess the changing needs of their birthparent and adoptive clients. For instance, adoption workers will have to be particularly sensitive to issues surrounding birthparents' and adoptive parents' feelings and fears about each other. During the adoption preparation period, it may be necessary to institute some kind of dialogue between potential adoptive families and birthparents, possibly in the form of group or panel discussions.

In addition, this study's findings indicate the parents who have confidential adoptions receive little birthparent information to pass along to their child. Agencies should therefore encourage adoptive families to preserve carefully, in a scrapbook or baby book, any information given to them. Should the need arise for more information, adoptive families must feel free to contact the agency at any time.

The findings also show that, once birthparents surrender a child for a confidential adoption, they tend to lose all contact with the agency. If future communication is to be fostered between adoptive families and the agency, the agency must educate birthparents of the necessity of placing accurate and complete medical and background information on *both* birth-parents in the child's files. Birthparents should also be offered the option of leaving letters or other kinds of nonidentifying information in the files, as well as be informed of any state or national adoption registries whose services they may wish to use in the future.

Any change in confidential adoption practice will take time and money and will create extra work for agency personnel. At first, some adoption workers and administrators may find change stressful. However, the resulting benefits to members of the adoption triad—birthparents, adoptive parents, and adopted children—will make change within agencies worth-while.

9
Conclusions

The interview data from 17 adoptive families and birthparents in this study strongly suggest that the degree of openness desirable in any particular case is a highly individual matter. No one type of adoption can be regarded as "best" for every family situation.

For some families, confidential adoptions may be problematic. As noted earlier in this book, children in confidential adoptions may feel cut off from their past and may experience identity problems, birthparents may go for many years with unresolved feelings of guilt and loss, and adoptive parents may feel insecure in their role because of the unknown future they anticipate with their child's birthparents.

Given the balance of the risks and values of openness in adoption, and the majority of adoptive and birth families who have appropriate preadoption counseling available to them, the greatest benefit and the least risk seems to occur in families with semiopen adoptions. This practice, which generally involves an exchange of nonidentifying information, pictures, letters, gifts, and possibly one face-to-face meeting involving no exchange of identities, seems less threatening to the integrity of the adoption triad and may be the easiest for adoption agencies to implement.

The theoretical perspectives that guided this investigation support this conclusion. In a semiopen adoption, the attachment and bonding between adoptive parent and child may be stronger without interference by birthparents. In addition, the adoptive parents would feel more secure if the parties involved did not exchange identifying information. The child may be more likely to feel that he is "matched" with his adoptive parents, if he or she is not constantly reminded of the contrast between birthparents and adoptive parents.

Cognitive developmental theory suggests that a child's understanding of adoption does not reach a mature level until adolescence. However, having some information about birthparents may facilitate the understanding of his or her own identity as an adopted child. Ongoing contact may serve to increase the complexity of the child's task, as he or she must construct not only a sense of self, but also an understanding of the birthparents.

Discrepant cognitions about being "given up" or "given away" by a birthmother who visits the home regularly may be avoided by a semiopen approach to adoptions practice. This will serve to minimize the opportunity for misunderstanding and confusion about the reasons for the child's placement.

Semiopen adoptions serve to promote Kirk's notion of acknowledgment of difference, without moving toward insistence of difference. This process also tends to minimize problems regarding role expectations of adoptive parents and birthparents.

Without the involvement of birthparents in the lives of adoptive families, family boundaries may be more stable, and family equilibrium may be preserved. A semiopen approach preserves and protects the adoptive family system from interruptions from birthparents, and normal family relationships can be fostered.

Moreover, in semiopen adoptions, adoptees have more complete information about birthparents than in confidential adoptions, but are not subjected to the possible confusion of roles among adoptive parents and birthparents that may occur in open adoptions. They are able to develop a more positive sense of self than if such data were unavailable, since they have information about, and possibly pictures of, their birthparents. Adoptive parents can avoid the interference of regular contact with birthparents, but have the security of knowing that if additional information is needed to help the child understand the adoption, birthparents would be easily accessible. Birthparents have the security of knowing about the status of the child and occasionally may be able to see pictures of the child and/or receive updates on the child's progress in the adoptive family.

Some families who begin with a semiopen adoption may later choose to increase the degree of contact with birthparents. The decision to move to fully disclosed openness should depend on a number of factors, including but not limited to the following:

ADOPTIVE PARENTS

—security in the parenting role

—ability to be assertive about maintaining family boundaries

—ability to cope with adopting not only a child, but possibly many relatives and an extended family network

—ability to deal with differing degrees of openness within their family, if they have more than one adopted child

BIRTHPARENTS

—resolution of grief at relinquishing rights to the child

—emotional maturity

—ability to acknowledge adoptive parents' legal rights to parent the child

—availability to spend time with the birthchild

ADOPTION AGENCIES

—availability of staff to serve as go-between for families corresponding through the agency

—availability of trained staff to provide ongoing educational and counseling services to families choosing fully disclosed openness

—financial resources for postadoption programs

Fully disclosed openness, while it has worked very well for some families (see vignettes in Chapter 6 about the Martin and Griffith families), presents many unanticipated challenges to all members of the adoption triad. The decision to move to fully disclosed openness should not be made lightly. As may be noted from the vignettes in Chapter 6, the decision to disclose commits adoptive parents to take on not only a child, but a whole new network of relatives. While the new network in some cases simply include the child's birthmother, in other cases it may encompass both birthparents, aunts, uncles, grandparents, and possibly new spouses and children of birthparents. The dynamics in such families are complex and share many of the same challenges that are being encountered in blended families and postdivorce families with joint custody. We strongly recommend that adoptive families engaged in fully disclosed openness maintain close ties with the postadoption program of their adoption agency and that they avail themselves of workshops and counseling as needed throughout the child's life, and not only in the early years of placement.

The findings of this study are limited by the availability sample of families from offices within one private adoption organization in the state of Texas, and should not be generalized to all adoption agencies or families. In order to test the reliability of the findings, we are currently engaged in a replication and extension of this study, using agencies throughout the United States and a much larger sample.

The sample selection process was also a methodological limitation of the study. Since birthparents first had to be matched with corresponding adoptive parents in order to be included in the study, and had to be contacted by letter or phone, only families who had kept in touch with the agency were selected for participation. Families who could easily be reached by the agency were likely to have had a very positive experience with their adoption and were more likely to volunteer to participate in the study. This self-selection process may have tended to bias the results in favor of finding greater satisfaction with the form of adoption that had been chosen.

We feel strongly that the consequences of openness for adopted children in this study remain unknown because the children were too young to be interviewed. A longitudinal follow-up of this sample on a regular basis is strongly recommended.

Finally, this study was an exploratory pilot project by design, and all of the findings must be interpreted as being suggestive rather than definitive, and are relevant only to this sample population.

10
Commentary

The development of the practice of openness in adoption was
really less dramatic and revolutionary than it may first appear. It did not come with suddenness, nor did it cause major
tremors throughout the agency system. It evolved over years
of trial, change, and response to client needs. While the latest
face-to-face meeting option of the openness practice did cause
more concern and required more planning, other options, such
as the birthmother's involvement in selecting the adoptive
parents or communication among the birthparents and adoptive parents through letters, have histories that date back as
far as ten years.

In order to assure that everyone understands open adoption
according to Lutheran Social Service of Texas' practice, I will
list all of the optional procedures that are available to our
clients. The birthparent has the option to spend time with the
baby, name the child on the original birth certificate, learn
the first name of the child and the first names of the adoptive
parents, participate in the selection of the adoptive parents,
have ongoing correspondence with the adoptive parents
(through the agency—no last names or addresses shared), share
pictures of him or herself and the extended family with adop-

tive parents, send a gift for the child, and meet in person with
the adoptive couple.

The adoptive parents have the option to learn the first
name(s) of birthparent(s), engage in ongoing correspondence,
send pictures of their child to the birthparent(s), obtain pictures of the birthparent(s) and extended family, obtain a more
complete social and medical history of birth families, and meet
in person with the birthparent(s). Clients may choose, with
staff concurrence, any or none of the above options.

The major concern that openness in adoption raises is related to the sharing of identifying information between the
birthparents and adoptive parents. Lutheran Social Service of
Texas (LSST) practices openness in adoption *without sharing
identifying information.* Many professionals and agencies have
somehow concluded that openness, especially the face-to-face
meetings, must include the sharing of identifying information.
LSST is most interested in and concerned with the impact
that the sharing of identifying information has on the adoption triad. This study is partially the result of this specific
concern.

The development and initiation of the face-to-face meetings
between birthparents and adoptive parents began in 1981 as
a pilot project in two of our regional service offices, San Antonio and Corpus Christi. There were two goals that staff hoped
to accomplish with this additional option to openness. First,
quality would be increased by providing more sensitive and
responsible services to meet the needs of the adoption triad;
and second, openness would make adoption a more acceptable
and livable option to birthmothers.

The project was given clear parameters and expectations.
These included: (1) The practice must be consistent with the
agency's total services and client commitment. (2) Face-to-face
meetings must be considered as an option within the total
practice of openness and never forced upon clients. (3) Face-
to-face meetings are to be performed within quality, responsible professional standards. This practice must not be seen
as a cure-all or treatment gimmick. (4) The practice will be
formally reviewed, and a decision made as to its continuation.
An inservice training presentation on face-to-face meetings was

held in the spring of 1982 by the agency regional directors. The presentation was made by the two regions piloting the practice and included a review of the extensive planning and preparation that had been done prior to implementation and during the time of the project, a step-by-step review of the process itself, and video tapes on the face-to-face meetings. As a result of the presentation, the practice was given approval for use throughout the agency.

An extensive public-information campaign was launched for the purpose of making both the public and other professionals more aware and informed of the practice. This gave us an opportunity to hear reactions that the practice elicited. Through the help of a national church organization, the agency managed to obtain personal interviews on several national TV programs, including "ABC's Evening News," "Good Morning America," the "Today Show," and the "Merv Griffin Show," along with numerous newspaper and magazine articles. The feedback received was most positive and encouraging. In fact, there have been surprisingly few people or organizations who have been resistive and/or negative to the practice.

In the summer of 1983, a task force was organized to study the practice further and to make a report and recommendations to the agency. Membership of this task force included two professionals from outside the agency, adoptive parents, a birthparent, an adopted adult, and agency staff. The task force conducted two surveys, one to determine client satisfaction among agency clients, and the other to determine the degree of openness practiced by 71 adoption agencies.

The work of the task force was completed in March, 1984. The recommendations included:

1. The agency should maintain and guarantee to its clients openness on an optional, not mandatory basis.

2. The agency should make a greater commitment to the provision of postadoption services.

3. The agency should address the impact of ongoing, face-to-face meetings among the birth and adoptive parents on the child, especially during the developmental age span of 2 to 16 years.

4. The agency needs to initiate a study that will evaluate the impact of openness on clients.

This last recommendation was acted upon by the agency board in May, with the allocation of the necessary funds to conduct this study.

With the completion of the study and the review of the report, the agency faced the task of listening to critical feedback from an objective source. Agency staff expressed concerns about the agency's practice image, consistency in practice among our decentralized offices, and acceptable definitions of the concept by the study team. The major concern related to the disproportionate number of subjects, 10 out of 17, who have revealed their identities to one another and have continued direct contact to some degree after placement.

The question of identifying information is a major concern. The agency went into the face-to-face portion of the practice with full knowledge that some clients would surely identify themselves to each other. Even though we provided structure and control to the process, and even though we did not encourage it, we knew that it was one of the risks. While we were willing to take that risk, we were also concerned as to the number who would identify themselves and what effect that would have on the adoption process.

Out of the first 281 placements in which the clients opted for face-to-face meetings, only 24 have had ongoing, identified contact with each other. This represents 8.5 percent of the total, which we feel is acceptable within the practice. It is important to remember that this group of clients is not left to drift or cope on their own, but are known to the staff and are involved in receiving services.

We are pleased with this preliminary study and feel very positive about the investment required to conduct it. The development and initiation of new service-delivery techniques require responsible preparation, practice, and evaluation. One of our major concerns is related to how we, and now other agencies, maintain responsible service standards and expectations in the practice of open adoption. For an agency to "jump on the open-adoption bandwagon," without adequate preparation or evaluation, will certainly jeopardize the practice and ill serve the client.

This preliminary study affirms and encourages openness in adoption. It also raises questions for which more data and information are needed. A full study will certainly help the practice come to terms with these questions. In the meantime, our practice must be a balance between creative responsiveness and responsible judgment. What seems to be beneficial and helpful in the immediate situation does not guarantee that it will remain so 5 to 15 years hence. Yet, to remain resistive and closed to the obvious benefits of openness is irresponsible and unprofessional. We must occasionally be reminded that adoption is a risky business and that failures in the services plan will occur, regardless of the degree of openness.

What do we see in the future? Openness has happened. The movement toward openness is obvious and the needs of clients dictate it. The questions that must be addressed will deal with how much openness is responsible; openness in relation to client need and the ability of the client to benefit from it; client choice and determination; and, especially, the question of the effects of identifying information on the adopted child. It is hoped that a full study will be forthcoming in the near future, as the result of this preliminary study. There are many questions that still need to be addressed, discussed, and answered. While the future is always somewhat cloudy, one thing is very clear—adoption will never be the same again.

The Reverend Calvin O. Goerdel, M.S.W.
Vice President for Social Services
Lutheran Social Service of Texas

Appendix A: Adoptive Parent Interview Schedule

Background Questions
1. Why did you decide to adopt?
2. What did you expect the adoption process to be like?
3. Please explain the process you went through to adopt _____?
4. How did you feel going through the process?
5. Did you have to prove infertility at the time of your adoption application?
6. What age or sex preference for a child did you have when you first applied to adopt?
7. (*If more than one adopted child*): Are any of your adopted children related to each other biologically? If so, please specify how.
8. (*If more than one adopted child*): Are any of the adopted children related to either adoptive parent? If so, please specify how.
9. What do you know about _____'s birthparents (both birth-mother and birthfather), specifically: (a) age at birth of child; (b) occupation; (c) education; (d) marital status; (e) nationality; (f) special interests or talents; (g) medical history; (h) reason for relinquishing _____; (i) physical or emotional problems; (j) circumstances of pregnancy and delivery? What do you know about the prenatal care of the birthmother?

10. What was _____'s birth weight?
11. Were there any birth siblings?
12. Is _____ aware of them?
13. Is your adoption of _____: (a) a stepparent adoption, (b) a foster parent adoption, (c) a transracial adoption, (d) an older child adoption, (e) an infant adoption, or (f) other (please specify): _____?
14. What other placements had _____ experienced before coming to your family? (Begin with birthparents). Type of placement (foster, adopt, etc.): (a) length, and (b) quality.
15. Was _____ ever abused or neglected in any of these placements? If so, please describe.
16. How old were you when _____ was adopted?
17. Were you adopted?
18. Do any of your friends have adopted children?
19. Do any of your relatives have adopted children?
20. How did your relatives react to your decision to adopt?

Open Adoption Questions
21. What options did your adoption agency offer regarding open or closed adoptions (e.g., nonidentifying information, continued sharing of information, meeting parents, ongoing contact, etc.)?
22. Had you heard of open adoptions before you came to LSST?
23. If so, what did you think the term meant?
24. What does the term "traditional adoption" mean to you?
25. Describe the process you went through before deciding what form of openness you would choose.
26. What option did you choose?
27. Why did you choose this option?
28. What advantages do you see in traditional adoption? open adoption?
29. What disadvantages do you see in traditional adoption? open adoption?

If Respondent Chose to Share Information Only
30. How often do you plan to share information with birthparents?
31. For what period of time?
32. What kind of information do you plan to share (pictures, gifts, etc.)?
33. What will the birthparents be sharing with you?

34. Is there a formal agreement for this kind of sharing?
35. What impact do you think sharing information will have on your child? on you and your spouse?; on birthparents? (*For older children*): What impact has this sharing had on the child? on you and your spouse? on birthparents?

If Respondent Chose to Meet Birthparents

36. Describe the circumstances of your first meeting. Did it occur at placement or later?
37. How did you feel during the meeting?
38. Did you exchange identifying information?
39. Why or why not?
40. What else did you talk about?
41. Do you plan to have continued contact?
42. What kind of an impact did the meeting have on you?
43. What kind of an impact did the meeting have on the birthparent(s)?
44. What kind of an impact do you think such meetings will have on the child?
45. What kind of a difference do you think this meeting will have on your family in the future?

If Respondent Chose to Have Ongoing Contact

46. Describe the circumstances of your first meeting.
47. What other contacts have you had with the birthparent(s)?
48. How would you describe your relationship with the birthparent(s)?
49. What has been the impact of these meetings on the child?
50. What do you think the impact will be as _____ grows up?
51. What do you think the impact will be on your family?
52. Does your child know what "birthmother" means?
53. What does the child call his/her birthmother?
54. How do you feel about this?
55. Are any of the birthparents' relatives (grandparents, aunts, uncles, etc.) involved in the child's life?
56. Do you ever fear that the birthmother might change her mind and wish to reclaim her child? What other fears do you have?
57. What kind of role do you want the birthparent to play in your family's life in three years? in six years? in ten years? in fifteen years? after the child reaches adulthood?

58. Do you ever seek the birthparent's advice? For what areas?
59. Do you consider the birthmother to be a part of your family? If so, how (relative, friend, etc.)?
60. What is the most satisfying aspect of your relationship with the birthparent(s)?
61. What is the most difficult aspect of this relationship?
62. Describe the birthparent(s)' relationship(s) with your child; with you.
63. Has the birthparent's relationship with you changed at all since placement? Why or why not? Describe.
64. Do you behave differently with your child in the presence of the birthparent?
65. How do you view the birthparent?
66. Has the birthparent ever said he/she regrets the decision to relinquish his/her child, and/or that he/she wants the child back?
67. Have you ever regretted making the decision to have an open adoption?

If Respondent Chose Traditional (Closed) Adoption

68. How do you plan to talk with your child about adoption? (*For older children*): How have you talked with your child about adoption: (a) now? (b) in middle childhood? (c) in adolescence?
69. What kinds of information do you think adoptive parents should have about their child's background? Why?
70. What kinds of information do you think adopted children should have about themselves? Why?
71. What kinds of information do you think birthparents should have about their children after they have been placed?
72. How would you handle it if your child decided to search for his/her birthparent(s)? Why?
73. What is the meaning of "open adoption" to you? What do you think the consequences of open adoption would be for the adoptive parents?; the adopted child?; the birthparent(s)?

Ask of All Respondents

74. How did your relatives react to the degree of openness you chose in your adoption?
75. How did your friends react to the degree of openness you chose in your adoption?

76. Have you told your child that he/she is adopted? What did you say? When?
77. What was _____'s reaction?
78. If not, when do you plan to tell your child? How?
79. How will you feel if your child wishes to contact birthparent(s) when he/she gets older? What would you do if they asked you to help them?
80. How many parent figures would you say _____ has?
81. Who are they?
82. Do you think that adoptive children can really belong to an adoptive family?
83. Do you feel that _____ really belongs to you?
84. What are some of the satisfactions you encountered in the type of adoption you chose?
85. What are some of the problems you encountered in the type of adoption you chose?
86. What do you think are the rights of adoptive parents?
87. What do you think are the rights of birthparents?
88. What to you think are the rights of adopted children?
89. How do you feel about traditional (closed) adoptions now?
90. How do you feel about open adoptions now?
91. (*If more than one adopted child*): How would you compare the experiences you had in adopting each of your children (satisfactions, difficulties, etc.)?
92. Do you belong to any adoptive parent groups?
93. Are you active in any community, cultural, or religious groups that you would view as supports for your role as parent? If so, please describe.
94. Do you believe that adoptive parents need to have some abilities in addition to those generally needed by good parents?
95. What are some of the joys and difficulties experienced by both adoptive parents and birthparents and adopted children and birthchildren?
96. Finally, given your experience as an adoptive parent, what advice would you give someone who is considering adoption?

Appendix B: Birthparent Interview Schedule

Background Questions
1. What were the circumstances that led to your decision to place your child for adoption?
2. What factors influenced your decision to place your child through Lutheran Social Service?
3. What did you expect the placement process to be like?
4. Please explain the process you went through to place _____.
5. How did you feel while going through the process?
6. What was your mother's reaction to your decision to place?
7. What was your father's reaction to this decision?
8. In what way, if any, has the baby's father been involved in your decision?
9. How old was _____ when he/she was placed?
10. Please describe your feelings during your hospital stay with the baby: Did you feed the baby? Did any members of your family come visit in the hospital? Were there any problems?
11. Did you name the baby?
12. Do you have other children? If so, please give ages.
13. Have you ever placed another child for adoption?
14. What do you know about _____'s adoptive parents (both

mother and father), specifically: (a) age at time of adoption; (b) occupation; (c) education; (d) marital status; (e) nationality/racial background; (f) special interests or talents; (g) medical history; (h) reason for adopting; and (i) personality characteristics?

15. Are there other children in the adoptive parents' home?
16. What else would you like to know about your child's adoptive parents?
17. What other placements had _____ experienced before being adopted by _____? (Did _____ ever live with you?) Type of placement (foster, adopt, etc.): (a) length, and (b) quality.
18. How old were you when _____ was placed for adoption?
19. Were you adopted?
20. Do any of your friends have adopted children?
21. Do any of your relatives have adopted children?
22. Please describe the experiences of friends or relatives who have adopted or placed children for adoption. How have they influenced your feelings?
23. How did your relatives react to your decision to place?
24. How did your friends react to your decision to place?

Open Adoption Questions
25. What options did your adoption agency offer regarding open or closed adoptions (nonidentifying information, continued sharing of information, meeting parents, ongoing contact, etc.)?
26. Had you heard of open adoptions before you came to LSST?
27. If so, what did you think the term meant?
28. What does the term "traditional or closed adoption" mean to you?
29. Describe the process you went through before deciding which form of openness you would choose: What were your feelings?; your concerns?
30. What options did you choose?
31. Why did you choose this option?
32. What advantages do you see in traditional adoption? open adoption?
33. What disadvantages do you see in traditional adoption? open adoption?

If Respondent Chose to Share Information Only
34. How often do you plan to share information with adoptive parents?

35. For what period of time?
36. What kind of information do you plan to share (pictures, gifts, etc.)?
37. What will the adoptive parents be sharing with you?
38. Is there a formal agreement for this kind of sharing?
39. What impact do you think sharing information will have on your child? on you (and your spouse, if married now)? on adoptive parents? (*For older children*): What impact has this sharing had on the child? on you and your spouse/companion? on adoptive parents?

If Respondent Chose to Meet Birthparents

40. Describe the circumstances of your first meeting. Did it occur at placement or later?
41. How did you feel during the meeting?
42. Did you exchange identifying information (first or last name, address, telephone number, etc.)?
43. Why or why not?
44. What else did you talk about?
45. Do you plan to have continued contact? Why or why not?
46. What kind of an impact did the meeting have on you?
47. What kind of an impact did the meeting have on the adoptive parents?
48. What kind of an impact do you think such meetings will have on the child?
49. What kind of a difference do you think this meeting will have on your family in the future?

If Respondent Chose to Have Ongoing Contact

50. Describe the circumstances of your first meeting (while pregnant; after delivery).
51. What other contacts have you had with the adoptive parent(s)?
52. How would you describe your relationship with the adoptive parents?
53. Do you ever feel like you are in competition with the adoptive parents?
54. What has been the impact of these meetings on the child?
55. What do you think the impact will be as _____ grows up?
56. What do you think the impact will be on you and your family?
57. Does your child know what "birthmother" means?
58. What does the child call you?

59. How do you feel about this?
60. What would you like for him/her to call you?
61. What does the child call his/her adoptive mother?
62. How do you feel about this?
63. Are any of your relatives involved in the child's life?
64. Do you wish you could reclaim your child? What other wishes or dreams do you have about you and your child?
65. What kind of role do you want to play in your child's life in three years? in six years? in ten years? in fifteen years? after the child reaches adulthood?
66. Does the adoptive mother or father ever seek your advice? On what issues or questions?
67. Do you consider yourself a part of your child's adoptive family? If so, how (relative, friend, etc.)?
68. Do you view _____ as being a part of your family?
69. What is the most satisfying aspect of your relationship with _____?
70. What is the most difficult aspect of your relationship with _____?
71. What is the most satisfying aspect of your relationship with your child's adoptive parents?
72. What is the most difficult aspect of your relationship with your child's adoptive parents?
73. Have the adoptive parents' relationships with you changed at all since placement? Why or why not? Describe.
74. How do you behave with your birthchild while in the presence of his/her adoptive parents?
75. How do you view the adoptive parents (as parents, as friends, etc.)?
76. Have you ever told the adoptive family that you regret the decision to relinquish your birthchild and/or that you want _____ back?
77. Have you ever regretted making the decision to have an open adoption?

If Respondent Chose Traditional (Closed) Adoption

78. How do you think adoptive parents should explain adoption to children: In early childhood? In middle childhood? In adolescence?

79. What kinds of information do you think adoptive parents should have about their child's background? Why?
80. What kinds of information do you think adopted children should have about their backgrounds?
81. What kinds of information do you think birthparents should have about their children after they have been placed?
82. What is the meaning of "open adoption" to you? What do you think the consequences of open adoption would be for the adoptive parent? the adopted child? the birthparent(s)?

Ask of All Respondents

83. How did your relatives react to the degree of openness you chose in your adoption?
84. How did your friends react to the degree of openness you chose in your adoption?
85. What do you think the term "adoption" means to a child?
86. How will you feel if your child wishes to contact you when he/she gets older?
87. How many parent figures would you say _____ has?
88. Who are they?
89. Do you think that adopted children can really belong to an adoptive family?
90. Do you feel that _____ really belongs to his/her adoptive family?
91. What are some of the satisfactions you encountered in the type of adoption you chose?
92. What are some of the problems you encountered in the type of adoption you chose?
93. What do you think are the rights of adoptive parents?
94. What do you think are the rights of birthparents?
95. What do you think are the rights of adopted children?
96. How do you feel about traditional (closed) adoptions now?
97. How do you feel about open adoptions now?
98. (*If placed more than one child for adoption*): How would you compare the experiences you had in placing each of your children for adoption? (satisfactions, difficulties, etc.)?
99. Do you belong to any birthparent support groups?
100. Are you active in any community, cultural, religious, or other groups that support you as a birthparent? If so, please describe.
101. Do you believe that adoptive parents need to have some abilities in addition to those generally needed by good parents?

102. What are some of the joys and difficulties experienced by both adoptive parents and birthparents and adopted children and birthchildren?
103. Finally, given your experience as a birthparent, what advice would you give someone who is considering placing a child for adoption?

References

Adoptees' Liberty Movement Association. *State registries—Solution . . . or advantage?* New York: Author.

Ainsworth, M. D. S. (1973). The development of infant-mother attachment. In B. M. Caldwell & H. N. Ricciuti (Eds.), *Review of child development research: Vol. 3.* Chicago: University of Chicago Press.

Ainsworth, M. D. S. (1979). Infant-mother attachment. *American Psychologist, 34,* 932–937.

Ainsworth, M. D. S. (1979). Strange situation.

Ainsworth, M. D. S., Blehar, M., Waters, E., & Wall, S. (1978). *Patterns of attachment.* Hillsdale, NJ: Erlbaum.

Amadio, C., & Deutsch, S. L. (1983). Open adoption: Allowing (11) • adopted children to "stay in touch" with blood relatives. *Journal of Family Law, 22* (1).

Andrews, R. G. (1978). Adoption: Legal resolution or legal fraud? *Family Process, 17,* 313–328.

Andrews, R. G. (1979). A clinical appraisal of searching. *Public Welfare, 37* (3), 15–21.

Arend, R., Gove, F. L., & Sroufe, L. A. (1979). Continuity of individual adaptation from infancy to kindergarten: A predictive study of ego-resiliency and curiosity in preschoolers. *Child Development, 50,* 950–959.

Baran, A., Pannor, R., and Sorosky, A. D. (1976). Open adoption. *Social Work, 21,* 97–100.

• Barth, R. (1987). Adolescent mothers' beliefs about open adoption. *Social Casework, 68,* 323–331.

• Belbas, N. (1987). Staying in touch: Empathy in open adoptions. *Smith College Studies in Social Work, 57,* 184–198.

Bernard, V. W. (1963). Adoption. In Albert Deutsch & Helen Fishman (Eds.), *Encyclopedia of Mental Health: Vol. 1.* New York: Watts.

Bertocci, D. H. (1978). On adoption. *Social Work, 23* (3).

• Borgman, R. (1982). The consequences of open and closed adoptions for older children. *Child Welfare, 61* (4), 217–226.

Bowlby, J. (1969). *Attachment and loss:* Vol. 1. New York: Basic Books.

Brieland, D., Costin, L., & Atherton, C. (1980). *Contemporary social work.* New York: McGraw-Hill.

Brinich, P. (1980). Some potential effects of adoption on self and object representations. In A. Solnit, R. Eissler, A. Freud, M. Kris, & P. Neubauer (Eds.), *The Psychoanalytic Study of the Child.* New Haven: Yale University Press.

Brinich, P., & Brinich, E. (1982). Adoption and adaptation. *The Journal of Nervous and Mental Disease, 170* (8), 489–493.

Broadhurst, D. D., & Schwartz, E. J. (1979). The right to know. *Public Welfare, 37* (3), 5–8.

Brodzinsky, D. M., Singer, L. M., & Braff, A. M. (1984). Children's understanding of adoption. *Child Development, 55,* 869–878.

Campbell, L. H. (1979). The birthparent's right to know. *Public Welfare, 37* (3), 22–27.

Child Welfare League of America. (1973). *Standards for adoption service* (rev. ed.). New York: Author.

Children's Home Society of California. (1984). *The changing picture of adoption.* Los Angeles: Author.

• Children's Home Society of Minnesota. (1981). *Openness in Adoption Pilot Project.* Unpublished Manuscript.

Cliff, K. (1983, September 16). Adoption law reviews mixed. *San Antonio Express.*

Clothier, F. (1943). The psychology of the adopted child. *Mental Hygiene, 27.*

Colgrove, W., Bloomfield, H., & McWilliams, P. (1976). *How to survive the loss of a love.* New York: Bantam.

Colon, F. (1978). Family ties and child placement. *Family Process, 17,* 289–312.

Cominos, H. (1971). Minimizing the risks of adoption through knowledge. *Social Work, 16* (1), 73–79.

Concerned United Birthparents, Inc. *The birthparents' perspective.* Milford, MA: Author.

Cordes, L. (1983). Changing adoption policy reflects need. [Speaking out]. *Midland Reporter-Telegram.*

Costin, L. (1972). *Child welfare: Policies and practices.* New York: McGraw-Hill.

Curtis, P. (1986). The dialectics of open versus closed adoption of infants. *Child Welfare, 65,* 437–445.

Deykin, R. Y., Campbell, L., & Patti, P. (1984). The postadoption experience of surrendering parents. *American Journal of Orthopsychiatry, 54* (2), 270–280.

DiGiulio, J. (1987). Assuming the adoptive parent role. *Social Casework, 68,* 561–566.

Dukette, R. (1984). Value issues in present day adoption. *Child Welfare, 63* (3).

Easson, W. M. (1973). Special sexual problems of the adopted adolescent. *Medical Aspects of Human Sexuality,* 92–105.

Egeland, B., & Farber, E. A. (1984). Infant-mother attachment: Factors related to its development and changes over time. *Child Development, 55,* 753–771.

Elbow, M., & Knight, M. (1987). Adoption disruption: Losses, transitions, and tasks. *Social Casework, 68,* 546–552.

Eldred, C., Rosenthal, D., Wender, P., Kity, S., & Jacobsen, B. (1976). Some aspects of adoption in selected samples of adult adoptees. *American Journal of Orthopsychiatry, 46* (2), 279–290.

Engles, F. (1972). The origin of the family, private property and the state. Lawrence & Wishart.

Erikson, E. H. (1950). *Childhood and society.* New York: Norton.

Festinger, L. (1957). *A theory of cognitive dissonance.* New York: Row, Peterson Publishers.

Festinger, L. (1964). *Conflict, decision, and dissonance.* Stanford, CA: Stanford University Press.

Fisher, F. (1973). *The search for Anna Fisher.* New York: Arthur Fields.

Flynn, L. (1979). A parent's perspective. *Public Welfare, 37* (3), 28–33.

Forest, D. L. (1983). Adoption: A give-and-take situation. *Midland Reporter-Telegram,* pp. 1E–4E.

Foster, A. (1979). Who has the 'right' to know? *Public Welfare, 37* (3), 34–37.

Frailberg, S. (1973, June). *Research in maternal deprivation and its implications for social work.* Paper presented at the Friends of the Virginia Frank Child Development Center.

Freud, S. (1950). Family romance. In J. Strachey (Ed.), *Collected Papers: Vol 5.* London: Hogarth Press.

Geissinger, S. (1984). Adoptive parents' attitudes toward open birth records. *Family Relations, 33,* 579–585.

* Gilling, M., & Rauch, P. (1979, June). Paper presented at a National Conference of Catholic Charities, Washington, D.C.

Goldenwicker, H. Van (1985, October). Paper presented at a National Conference on Post Legal Adoption Services, Minneapolis, MN.

Grotevant, H. D., McRoy, R. G., & Jenkins, V. Y. (in press). *Emotionally disturbed adopted adolescents: Early patterns of family adaptation. Family Process.*

Groth, M., Bonnardel, D., Denis, D., Martin, J., & Vousden, H. (1987). An agency moves toward open adoption of infants. *Child Welfare, 66,* 248–257.

Halverson, K., & Hess, K. M. (1980). *The Wedded Unmother.* Minneapolis, MN: Augsburg Publishing House.

Harrington, J. D. (1979). Legislative reform moves slowly. *Public Welfare, 37,* (3), 49–57.

Hazen, N. L., & Durrett, M. E. (1982). Relationship of security of attachment to exploration and cognitive mapping abilities in 2-year-olds. *Developmental Psychology, 18,* 751–759.

Holland, J. L. (1973). *Making vocational choices: A theory of careers.* Englewood Cliffs, NJ: Prentice-Hall.

Holland, J. L. (1985). *Making vocational choices: A theory of vocational personalities and work environments.* (2nd ed.). Englewood Cliffs, NJ: Prentice-Hall.

Horn, J. M. (1983). The Texas adoption project: Adopted children and their intellectual resemblance to biological and adoptive parents. *Child Development, 54,* 268–275.

Humphrey, M. (1969). *The hostage seekers.* New York: Humanities Press.

Hunt, J. McV. (1961). *Intelligence and experience.* New York: Ronald Press.

Jaffee, B., & Fanshel, D. (1970). *How they fared in adoption: A follow-up study.* New York: Columbia University Press.

Jewett, C. (1978). *Adopting the older child.* Boston: Harvard Common Press.

Jones, M. A. (1976). *The sealed adoption record controversy: Report of a survey of agency policy, practice, opinion.* New York: Research Center, Child Welfare League of America, Inc.

Kadushin, A. (1974). *Child welfare services.* New York: Macmillan Publishing Co.

Kelly, C. (1984, May 17). Open adoption. *The Dallas Morning News,* pp. 1C–3C.

Kirk, H. D. (1959). A dilemma of adoptive parenthood: Incongruous role obligations. *Marriage and Family Living, 21* (4), 316–328.

Kirk, H. D. (1964). *Shared fate: A theory of adoption and mental health.* New York: Free Press.

Kirk, H. D. (1981). *Adoptive kinship: A modern institution in need of reforms.* Toronto: Butterworth Co.

Kirk, H. D., & McDaniel, S. (1984). Adoption policy in Great Britain and North America. *Journal of Social Policy, 13,* 75–84.

Kowal, K. A., & Schilling, K. M. (1985). Adoption through the eyes of adult adoptees. *American Journal of Orthopsychiatry, 55* (3), 354–362.

Kraft, A. D., Palombo, J., Mitchell, D. L., Woods, P. K., & Schmidt, A. W. (1985a). Some Theoretical Considerations on Confidential Adoptions I: The Birth Mother. *Child & Adolescent Social Work, 2* (1). New York: Human Sciences Press.

———. (1985b). Some Theoretical Considerations on Confidential Adoptions II: The Adoptive Parent. *Child & Adolescent Social Work, 2* (2). New York: Human Sciences Press.

Kraft, A. D., Palombo, J., Mitchell, D. L., Woods, P. K., Schmidt, A. W., & Tucker, N. G. (1985c). Some Theoretical Considerations on Confidential Adoptions III: The Adopted Child. *Child & Adolescent Social Work, 2* (3). New York: Human Sciences Press.

———. (1986). Some Theoretical Considerations on Confidential Adoptions IV: Countertransference. *Child & Adolescent Social Work, 3* (1). New York: Human Sciences Press.

Krugman, D. D. (1967). Differences in the relation of parents and children to adoption. *Child Welfare, 46* (5), 267–271.

Lerner, R. (1985). *On the origins of human plasticity.* Cambridge: at the University Press.

Lifton, B. J. (1975). *Twice born: Memoirs of an adopted daughter.* New York: McGraw-Hill.

Lifton, B. J. (1979). *Lost and found: The adoption experience.* New York: The Dial Press.

Lindsay, J. W. (1987). *Open adoption: A caring option.* Buena Park, CA: Morning Glory Press.

Lutheran Social Service of Texas, Inc. (1982, July). *Open adoption statement.* San Antonio, TX: Author.

Matas, L., Arend, R. A., & Sroufe, L. A. (1978). Continuity of adaptation in the second year: The relationship between quality of attachment and later competence. *Child Development, 49,* 547–556.

McRoy, R. G., & Zurcher, L. A. (1983). *Transracial adoptees: The adolescent years.* Springfield, IL: Charles C. Thomas Publishers.

McWhinnie, A. M. (1967). *Adopted children: How they grow up.* London: Routledge and Kegan Paul.

Mech, E. (1986). Pregnant adolescents: Communicating the adoption option, *Child Welfare, 65,* 555–567.

Millen, L., & Roll, S. (1984). Solomon's mothers: A special case of pathological bereavement. *American Journal of Orthopsychiatry, 54* (2), 271–280.

Minuchin, S. (1974). *Families and family therapy.* Cambridge, MA: Harvard University Press.

Morrison, E. (1983, March). Breaking the seal. *New Jersey Reporter,* pp. 1–6.

National Committee for Adoption. (1985). *Adoption factbook: United States data, issues, regulations and resources.* Washington, DC: Author.

Pannor, R. (1985). Paper presented at a national Conference on Post Legal Adoption Services, Minneapolis, MN.

• Pannor, R., & Baran, A. (1984). Open adoption as standard practice. *Child Welfare, 63* (3), 245–250.

Pannor, R., & Nerlove, E. A. (1977). Fostering understanding between adolescents and adoptive parents through group experiences. *Child Welfare, 56* (8), 537–545.

Pastor, D. L. (1981). The quality of mother-infant attachment and its relationship to toddlers' initial sociability with peers. *Developmental Psychology, 17,* 326–335.

Paton, J. M. (1968). *Orphan voyage.* New York: Vantage.

Peller, L. (1963). Further comments on adoption. *Bulletin of the Philadelphia Association for Psychoanalysis, 13,* (1).

Pierce, W. L. (Producer). (1983). "Adoption Film" [Film]. San Antonio: Lutheran Social Service of Texas, Inc.

Polansky, N. (Ed.). (1975). *Social work research: Methods for the helping professions* (rev. ed.). Chicago: University of Chicago Press.

Raynor, L. (1980). *The adopted child comes of age.* London: Allen Publications.

Reynolds, W., Levey, C., & Eisnits, M. (1978, March). Adoptees' personality characteristics and self-ratings of adoptive family life. *Journal of Eastern Psychological Association.*

Rillera, M. J., & Kaplan, S. (1985). *Cooperative adoption: A handbook*. Westminster, CA: Triadoption Publications.

Ryburn, M. (1987). Open adoption. *New Zealand Social Work Journal, 11*, 2–7.

Rynearson, E. K. (1982). Relinquishment and its maternal complications: A preliminary study. *American Journal of Psychiatry, 139*, (3), 338–340.

Sachdev, P. (1984). *Adoption: Current issues and trends*. Toronto: Butterworth and Co.

Sanders, P., & Sitterly, N. (1981). *Search aftermath and adjustments*. Costa Mesa, CA: ISC Publications.

Sants, H. (1964). Genealogical bewilderment in children with substitute parents. *British Journal of Medical Psychology 37*, 133–141.

Scarr, S., & Weinberg, R. A. (1983). The Minnesota adoption studies: Genetic differences and malleability. *Child Development, 54*, 260–267.

Schecter, D. M. (1980). Observations on adopted children. *Archives of General Psychiatry, 3*, 21–32.

Schwartz, E. M. (1970). The family romance fantasy in children adopted in infancy. *Child Welfare, 49* (2), 386–391.

Seglow, J., Pringle, M. K., & Wedge, P. (1972). *Growing up adopted*. England & Wales: National Foundation for Educational Research.

Silber, K., & Speedlin, P. (1982). *Dear birthmother: Thank you for your baby*. San Antonio: Corona Publishing Co.

Small, J. W. (1979). Discrimination against the adoptee. *Public Welfare, 37* (3), 38–43.

Smith, J., & Miroff, F. I. (1981). *You're our child*. New York: University Press of America.

Sorich, C., & Siebert, R. (1982). Toward humanizing adoption. *Child Welfare, 61* (4), 207–216.

Sorosky, A. D., Baran, A., & Pannor, R. (1974). Adoptive parents and the sealed records controversy. *Social Casework, 55* (9), 531–536.

Sorosky, A. D., Baran, A., & Pannor, R. (1975). Identity conflicts in adoptees. *American Journal of Orthopsychiatry, 45* (1), 18–27.

Sorosky, A. D., Baran, A., & Pannor, R. (1978). *The adoption triangle*. New York: Anchor Press/Doubleday.

Sroufe, L. A., & Waters, E. (1977). Attachment as an organizational construct. *Child Development, 48*, 1184–1199.

Steinglass, P. (1987). A systems view of family interaction and psychopathology. In T. Jacob (Ed.), *Family interaction and psychopathology* (pp. 25–26). New York: Plenum.

Thomas, C. (1985, October). Paper presented at a National Conference on Post Legal Adoption Services, Minneapolis, MN.

Tighe, P. (1987). Searching for the past: Austin adoptees face tough choices. *Austin Family, 2,* 40–42.

Toussing, P. W. (1971). Realizing the potential in adoptions. *Child Welfare, 50* (6), 322–327.

Triseliotis, J. B. (1973). *In search of origins: The experiences of adopted people.* Boston: Routledge and Kegan Paul.

Ward, M. (1981). Parental bonding in older-child adoptions. *Child Welfare, 60* (1), 24–34.

Watson, K. W. (1979). Who is the primary client? *Public Welfare, 37* (3), 11–14.

Zeilinger, R. (1979). The need versus the right to know. *Public Welfare, 37* (3), 44–48.

Zill, N. (1985, April). *Achievement and behavior problems among adoptive children: Findings from a National Health Survey of Children.* Paper presented at the meeting of the Society for Research in Child Development, Toronto.

Author Index

Subject Index

acknowledgement of differences, 2, 11, 41-42
adolescence, as an issue in open placements, 21, 27-28
Adoptees' Liberty Movement Association (ALMA), 8-9, 13
adopted child (*see* children)
adoptive parents: acknowledgment of differences, 11, 41-42; attitude toward open records, 11; benefits of openness for, 20-21, 31, 69, 117 (*see* fully disclosed adoption, benefits and semiopen adoption, benefits); guilt toward birthmother, 35, 80, 109; infertility in, 2, 28; rights, 77, 80, 90; risks of openness for, 26-29, 39-41, 47, 117-18 (*see* fully disclosed adoption, risks and semiopen adoption, risks); role handicap, 2, 41
adoption: agency views, 67; defi-

nition, 1, 18-19; revelation, 6, 37; societal views, 2, 4, 10; statistics, 1
agencies: history of openness, 15-18; post-placement role in openness, 12-13, 19, 76, 86, 88, 120-23, 128; practice of openness, 15-16, 67-69; preparation of triad for openness, 109, 119-24, 127-28
Attachment theory, 33-35; application to adoption relationship, 28-29, 34-35, 118, 126; definition, 33

birthparents: adjustment to relinquishment, 12, 17, 20-21, 114; anonymity, wish for, 12; attitudes toward open records, 12; benefits of openness for 17, 21, 68 (*see* fully disclosed adoption, benefits, and semiopen adoption, benefits); mo-

About the Authors

RUTH G. McROY, Ph.D., is an Associate Professor of Social Work at the University of Texas at Austin. She coauthored the book, *Transracial and Inracial Adoptees: The Adolescent Years*, has published numerous articles, and has made presentations throughout the country on such topics as transracial adoptions, postadoption services, racial identity development, and open adoptions.

HAROLD D. GROTEVANT, Ph.D., is Professor of Home Economics and Psychology and Head of the Division of Child Development and Family Relationships at the University of Texas at Austin. His research focuses on identity formation, family communication processes, relationships in normal and troubled adoptive families, and the consequences of openness in adoptions. He has published over 60 articles and has presented his work at national and international conferences.

KERRY L. WHITE, M. A., is the Head Teacher at Hyde Park Baptist Child Development Center in Austin, Texas. While completing her master's degree in Child Development, she served as Research Associate to Ruth G. McRoy and Harold D. Grotevant.